BEST
COOKIES
cookbook

WILEY

Wiley Publishing, Inc.

GENERAL MILLS

Editorial Director: Jeff Nowak

Manager and Editor, Cookbooks: Lois Tlusty

Recipe Development and Testing: Pillsbury Kitchens

Photography: General Mills Photography Studios and Image Library

Photographer: Chuck Nields

Food Stylists: Barb Standel, Karen Linden

Prop Stylist: Michele Joy

WILEY PUBLISHING, INC.

Publisher: Natalie Chapman

Executive Editor: Anne Ficklen

Editor: Adam Kowit

Production Editor: Jacqueline Beach

Cover Design: Suzanne Sunwoo

Art Direction and Design: Tai Blanche

Layout: Indy Composition Services

Photography Art Direction: Chris Everett

Manufacturing Manager: Kevin Watt

Home of the Pillsbury Bake-Off© Contest

Pillsbury

Our recipes have been tested
in the Pillsbury Kitchens and meet our
standards of easy preparation, reliability
and great taste.

For more great recipes visit
pillsbury.com

Library of Congress Cataloging-in-Publication Data:
Pillsbury best cookies cookbook / Pillsbury editors.
    p. cm.
    Includes index.
    ISBN 978-0-470-40738-7 (cloth : alk. paper) 1. Cookies. I. Pillsbury Company. II. Title: Best cookies cookbook.
    TX772.P478 2009
    641.8'654—dc22

                      2008038583

Printed in China

10 9 8 7 6 5 4 3 2 1

Cover photo: S'more Thumbprint Cookies (page 42), Iced Lemon Cookies (page 36), and Mint-Kissed Meringues (page 28)

Welcome . . .

From the Pillsbury Kitchens
Home of the Pillsbury Bake-Off® Contest

Cookies—the perfect treat.

They're easy to make, **easy** to eat and easy to **love**—
what could be more **perfect**?

*Pillsbury **Best Cookies Cookbook*** has cookies and bars for any
occasion. Family **favorites** for filling the **cookie jar**, treats to
share during the holidays and scrumptious **brownies** and bars
to enjoy with **family** and **friends**.

Check out the "**easy**" cookies that start with refrigerated cookie
dough or brownie mix. No one will know you had a little "help" in the
kitchen. And only Pillsbury can share an entire chapter of winning
Bake-Off® cookies and bars with you.

Cookies bring back **memories** for many of us. Baking and decorating
holiday cookies with Mom or Grandma. Sneaking cookies from the
cookie jar with Grandpa. Remember when you baked your first batch of
cookies and everyone **raved** about them?

Now's the perfect time to bake up a batch of cookies and create new
memories!

Warmly,

Lois Tlusty

Pillsbury Editor

CONTENTS

cookie notes

Baking cookies and bars is basically easy, but have you asked "What is the best cookie sheet to buy?" or "Why is this cookie dough so soft and sticky?" Here you'll find the answers to these questions and more that will help make your baking experience even more enjoyable.

Ingredients and Equipment

Selecting and understanding the ingredients is the first step to baking great cookies and bars. And using the correct equipment is as important as using the best ingredients.

Cookie and Bar Ingredients

Flour: Most cookie and bar recipes call for *all-purpose flour.* Either bleached or unbleached can be used. *Whole wheat flour* will produce satisfactory cookies and bars. For best results, use half all-purpose and half whole wheat flour.

Fats: These add tenderness and moistness to cookies and bars. *Butter* offers more flavor, but either butter or *regular margarine* (not whipped or low-fat spreads) can be used. Regular or butter-flavored *shortening* can also be used and is interchangeable with butter or margarine.

Baking Powder and Baking Soda: *Baking soda* needs an acidic ingredient, such as brown sugar, molasses, sour cream or chocolate, to react. *Baking powder* contains baking soda and just the right amount of acid to produce its own leavening power.

Eggs: Eggs add richness, moisture and structure to cookies and bars. Recipes in this cookbook were tested using large eggs.

Sugars: *Sugar* adds sweetness, tenderness and moisture to cookies and bars and aids in browning. When "sugar" is listed in the ingredient list, it means granulated sugar. *Brown sugar* not only adds sweetness but also color to cookies and bars.

Baking Equipment

Most cookie and bar recipes require very little equipment. But if you love to make cookies, you may have a few special gadgets, such as a cookie press to make spritz cookies or a variety of fun cookie cutters.

Wooden or Plastic Mixing Spoons: These are sturdy for mixing doughs and have long handles that are comfortable to hold.

Hand or Stand Mixers: They are good for beating butter, sugar and eggs. Flour and other dry ingredients are best beaten in on low speed or stirred in with a spoon so they don't fly out of the bowl.

Measuring Cups and Spoons: Use to accurately measure ingredients, which is key to baking success. Use *nested "dry-ingredient" measuring cups* to measure ingredients where you need to level off the top. Use a *glass or plastic liquid measuring cup* with a pour spout and space above the top printed measurement for liquids.

Cooling Racks: Purchase racks that rise at least ½ inch above the surface of your countertop so air can circulate around the cookies or pan. Select racks with wires placed closely together so delicate or small cookies won't fall through.

Cookie Sheets

Having three or four cookie sheets is ideal, so that as one sheet is baking, you have another cooled sheet to get ready for the oven. Purchase cookie sheets that are at least 2 inches narrower and shorter than the inside of your oven, so the heat will circulate around them.

Basically, four types of cookie sheets are available. When purchasing cookie sheets, it is good to understand how each type performs.

Shiny Aluminum: Silver-colored aluminum cookie sheets without sides or with one side are the best. They reflect the heat so cookies bake evenly without the bottoms becoming too dark before they are done. If the cookie sheet is thin and the cookie edges and bottoms are becoming too dark, put two sheets together for added insulation.

Insulated: Also called cushioned or double-layered cookie sheets, these have a layer of air between two sheets of metal. Cookies do not brown as much on the bottom, which can make doneness harder to judge. In addition, the baking time increases slightly.

Dark Nonstick: There is no need to grease these cookie sheets, but the darker surface absorbs heat so the bottoms of cookies may be too dark and hard. For better results, reduce the oven temperature by 25° and rotate cookie sheets during baking for even browning.

Black Surface: Cookies bake faster on dark, nonreflective surfaces, which absorb heat, so watch the cookies closely and check for doneness at the minimum bake time to prevent the bottoms from burning. Reducing the oven temperature by 25° also helps prevent the bottoms from becoming too dark and the tops too brown.

Baking Pans

Baking pans for bars and brownies are available in different sizes and materials. Always use the size pan specified in the recipe. Bars baked in a pan that is too large become hard and overbaked, and in a pan too small can be doughy in the center and hard on the edges.

Shiny Metal: These are preferred because they reflect the heat and help prevent the edges and corners from becoming too brown and hard.

Dark Nonstick: No need to grease these pans, but the dark surface absorbs heat, so bars and brownies may overbake and the edges and corners become hard. Follow the manufacturer's directions or reduce the oven temperature by 25°.

Glass Baking Dish: These absorb heat rather than reflect heat, so reducing the oven temperature by 25° and checking for doneness 3 to 5 minutes before the minimum bake time are good ideas.

Baking Cookies and Bars

Once the ingredients are measured and mixed together, it is time to bake the cookies or bars and enjoy the results. Here are some tips to ensure a great batch.

Grease with Spray or Shortening

Many cookie and bar recipes call for greasing the cookie sheet or baking pan to help prevent the cookies or bars from sticking to the pan. Grease the cookie sheet or pan (or just the bottom of the pan) only if the recipe specifies to do so; some recipes have a high proportion of fat and don't require a greased pan. When a recipe calls for cooking spray, shortening can also be used. Some recipes, such as meringue-type cookies, will specify using cooking parchment paper on the cookie sheet.

It is best to use cooking spray or shortening rather than butter or margarine, which can burn. Spray the cookie sheet or pan lightly but evenly with cooking spray, or use a pastry brush or a piece of paper towel or waxed paper to rub a thin layer of shortening over the sheet or pan.

Preheat the Oven

Always preheat the oven to be sure it's the proper temperature before baking the first sheet of cookies. Place the oven rack in the middle of the oven before turning on the oven. Allow at least 10 minutes to reach the desired temperature. Using an oven thermometer is a good idea to ensure an accurate temperature.

Bake a Test Cookie

Baking one "test" cookie is a good way to check if the dough is the correct consistency. If the cookie spreads too much, add 1 to 2 tablespoons flour to the dough or chill it for an hour or two. If the cookie is too dry and hard, add 1 to 2 tablespoons milk (or liquid specified in the recipe) to the dough.

Make Same-Size Cookies

Make all cookies the same size so they bake evenly. Cookies that are smaller than the others will become too brown or burn, and larger cookies won't be done in the center. A good way to make drop cookies the same size is to use a spring-handled cookie or ice-cream scoop. Use the size of scoop that's equal to the amount of dough specified in the recipe. Two common sizes are #70 scoop, which is equivalent to 1 level tablespoon, and #16 scoop, which is ¼ cup.

Bake One Sheet at a Time

For best results, bake one cookie sheet at a time on the middle oven rack. If you must bake two at a time, place the oven racks as close to the middle of the oven as possible. So cookies bake and brown evenly, switch the top cookie sheet with the bottom cookie sheet about halfway through the bake time, and turn the cookie sheets around.

Use Cooled Cookie Sheets

Always start with a cool cookie sheet. Dough baked on a hot or warm sheet becomes soft and spreads before the outside of the cookie has baked enough to hold its shape. If you don't have enough cookie sheets to allow them to cool between batches, you can cool the sheets quickly by placing them in the freezer or refrigerator for a few minutes. Or run cold water over them, dry completely and grease again if needed.

Doneness Test

Most recipes for cookies and bars specify a range for baking times to compensate for variations in ovens, equipment and ingredients. Check for doneness at the minimum time, looking for cookies that are firmly set or browned according to the recipe directions. When you touch them lightly with your finger, almost no imprint will remain. Follow the doneness test for bars as directed in the recipe.

Cooling Cookies and Bars

Most baked cookies should stay on the cookie sheet for a minute or two so they firm up and are easier to handle. If a recipe specifies to remove the cookies immediately, it is best to do so or they will stick to the sheet. Use a turner or pancake turner to move individual cookies from the cookie sheet to the cooling rack.

To cool bars and brownies, place the entire pan on a cooling rack for better air circulation.

Altitude Adjustments

When baking cookies or bars at altitudes over 3,500 feet above sea level, the results may not always be satisfactory. As the altitude increases, air pressure decreases, altering the way leavening agents, sweeteners and liquids interact. To ensure good results, all the recipes in this cookbook have been tested at high altitude (above 3,500 feet). See the High Altitude instructions following each recipe to see if specific changes are necessary or no adjustments are needed.

Storing Cookies and Bars

Cookies and bars will stay fresh longer if they are stored properly. Crisp cookies and soft cookies shouldn't be stored together. Also store different flavors in separate containers, or they will pick up the flavors of the other cookies.

Soft and Chewy Cookies: Store in a tightly covered container, such as plastic food containers with tight-fitting lids, metal tins, resealable food-storage plastic bags and cookie jars with screw-on lids or sealed-gasket lids.

Crisp Cookies: Store in a container with a loosely fitting cover, such as a cookie jar without a screw-on or sealed-gasket lid or a casserole dish with a lid. If the weather is very humid, it is better to store them in a container with a tight-fitting lid. If cookies have softened, heat them on a cookie sheet in a 300°F oven for 3 to 5 minutes, then cool them on a cooling rack.

Frosted or Decorated Cookies: Allow the frosting or decorations to become set or harden at room temperature before storing the cookies. Store cookies between layers of waxed paper, cooking parchment paper or foil in tightly sealed containers.

Bars and Brownies: Store in the baking pan covered with the pan lid or foil.

Freezing Baked Cookies and Bars

Place **unfrosted baked** cookies and cut bars in a freezer container with a tight-fitting lid or resealable freezer plastic bag; label the container and freeze up to 6 months. Or freeze one or two cookies or bars in a small resealable food-storage plastic bag, which can easily be popped into a lunch bag for a snack. **Meringue-type** and **custard- or cream-filled** cookies do not freeze well.

Freeze **frosted baked cookies** uncovered on a cookie sheet until hard. Then package the frozen cookies between layers of waxed paper or cooking parchment paper in a container with tight-fitting lid and freeze up to 3 months.

Thaw **soft-textured cookies** and bars in the storage container at room temperature. Remove **crisp-textured** cookies from the container and thaw at room temperature.

Storing Unbaked Cookie Dough

Store unbaked cookie dough tightly covered in the refrigerator for up to 24 hours. Batches of unbaked dough can be tightly wrapped in waxed paper, plastic wrap or foil and placed in a resealable freezer plastic bag or freezer container; label and freeze up to 6 months. Thaw frozen dough in the refrigerator about 8 hours before baking. If the thawed dough is still too stiff, let stand at room temperature until workable.

Freeze individual drops of cookie dough on cookie sheets. When dough is frozen, place the individual pieces in a resealable freezer plastic bag or freezer container; label and freeze up to 6 months. Place the frozen cookie dough pieces on a cookie sheet and bake at the temperature indicated in the recipe but add a few minutes to the bake time.

Sending Cookies and Bars

A package of homemade cookies or bars is always welcomed, whether it is sent to someone at a military base, a college student, a family member or a friend. Here are some tips for sending cookies and bars so they arrive in good condition (although a box of broken cookies will taste just as good).

- Moist, firm-textured cookies are best for sending because they will remain fresh and intact during shipping. Good choices include drop cookies, unfrosted bars, fudgy brownies and other sturdy cookies. Delicate, intricately shaped cookies are best for personal delivery.

- Line a firm-sided cardboard box, metal tin or plastic container with plastic wrap or foil for extra protection and to prevent cookies from absorbing odors. Layer the cookies between layers of waxed paper in the container. Or wrap cookies and bars in pairs, back to back, with plastic wrap or foil, and place them flat or on end in the container. Insulate the sides of the container with a "wall" of crumpled waxed paper or cooking parchment paper.

- For extra protection, place the container in a larger box padded on all sides with crumbled newspaper, bubble wrap, packing peanuts or other packing material. Be sure there is an inch or two of padding on the bottom and top of the container, too, so it doesn't move inside the packing box.

- Seal the packing box with shipping tape, and put a piece of transparent tape over the address label. Mark the box "perishable" so it is handled with care during shipping.

Storing Refrigerated Cookie Dough

Refrigerated cookie dough is great to have on hand when that "must have a cookie" urge hits. But it can also be used as a time-saving ingredient as a base for making delicious homemade cookies. It is best to use the dough before the "use-by" date on the package. If you don't use all the dough at one time, wrap the unused portion in plastic wrap or place in resealable plastic freezer bag and refrigerate up to 1 week or freeze up to 2 months. If the dough has been left out of the refrigerator more than two hours, be sure to discard.

Cookie and Bar Q&A

So, you measured, mixed and baked following the directions, but the results still aren't quite right. Read these Q&As for solutions to common problems.

Q: Why is the dough sticky and unworkable?

A: Chill the dough until it's firm enough to handle, about an hour. If it's still sticky, work in more flour, a tablespoon at a time, until the consistency improves.

Q: Why won't the dough hold together?

A: Work in additional milk or liquid called for in the recipe, a tablespoon at a time, until dough holds together. Or work in additional softened butter, margarine or shortening.

Q: Why do cookies bake together?

A: Make sure the cookie sheet is cool before placing the dough on it. A dough made with butter may spread more, so place the cookies further apart to allow for possible spreading.

Q: Why are the cookies overly flat and thin?

A: Use a cool cookie sheet to prevent the fat in the dough from melting too soon. Do not overgrease the cookie sheet. Be sure the butter isn't too soft if the recipe calls for softened butter. (It should give gently to pressure and leave a slight indentation.)

Q: Why are my rolled cookies tough?

A: Handle the dough gently and as little as necessary. Use as little flour as possible on the rolling pin and work surface. And don't reroll the dough scraps more than twice.

Q: Why do cookies stick to the cookie sheet?

A: They may have been left on the cookie sheet too long after being removed from the oven. Return the cookies to the oven for about 30 seconds to rewarm and loosen them. For the next batch, lightly grease the cookie sheet, or use a clean cookie sheet.

Q: Why do the cookies break when removed from the cookie sheet?

A: Let cookies cool and firm up for a minute or two before removing. Handle them carefully, and use a turner or pancake turner with a wide, thin blade to get under the cookie easily an d support it fully.

Q: Why are the cookies too dark or burned on the bottoms?

A: Use a shiny cookie sheet and watch the bake time closely. Bake one sheet at a time on the middle rack of the oven, and rotate the cookie sheet halfway through the bake time.

Q: Why do the cookies bake unevenly?

A: Be sure the cookies are the same size and spaced uniformly apart. Bake one sheet at a time in the middle of the oven, and rotate the cookie sheet halfway through the bake time. If you bake two sheets at a time, switch the top and bottom sheets halfway through baking and rotate them.

Q: Why do brownies crumble when cut?

A: Cool bars and brownies completely in the pan before cutting. Brownies and some soft and sticky bars cut better with a plastic knife.

Q: Why are the bars dry and hard?

A: Use the right size pan. Make sure the oven isn't too hot, and check for doneness at the minimum bake time. To avoid excess flour, spoon the flour into the measuring cup to avoid packing it down. Spread the dough evenly in the pan. If using a dark pan or glass baking dish, reduce the oven temperature by 25° and check bars 3 to 5 minutes before the minimum bake time.

(top left) Secret-Center Cookie Cups, page 40; *(top right)* Chocolate Chip Cookies, page 20; *(bottom)* S'more Thumbprint Cookies, page 42

family favorite cookies

caramel-frosted banana drops

Prep Time: 1 Hour 45 Minutes
Start to Finish: 1 Hour 45 Minutes

About 5 dozen cookies

COOKIES
1 cup packed brown sugar
1 cup butter or margarine,
    softened
½ cup mashed banana (1 large)
2 teaspoons vanilla
2⅓ cups all-purpose flour
¼ teaspoon salt
¾ cup chopped walnuts or pecans

FROSTING
¾ cup packed brown sugar
¼ cup butter or margarine,
    softened
1¼ cups powdered sugar
½ teaspoon vanilla
1 to 3 tablespoons milk

1 Heat oven to 350°F. In large bowl, beat 1 cup brown sugar and 1 cup butter with electric mixer on medium speed until light and fluffy. Beat in banana and 2 teaspoons vanilla until blended. On low speed, beat in flour and salt until well blended. Stir in walnuts.

2 On ungreased cookie sheets, drop dough by rounded teaspoonfuls 2 inches apart.

3 Bake 9 to 14 minutes or until light golden brown. Immediately remove from cookie sheets to cooling racks. Cool completely, about 30 minutes.

4 In 1-quart saucepan, heat ¾ cup brown sugar and ¼ cup butter over medium heat, stirring constantly, until sugar is dissolved. Cool slightly. Stir in powdered sugar, ½ teaspoon vanilla and enough milk until frosting is smooth and spreadable. Frost cookies. If frosting begins to thicken, stir in additional milk, 1 teaspoon at a time.

High Altitude (3500–6500 ft): Decrease brown sugar in cookies to ¾ cup. Increase flour to 2⅔ cups.

■■■ **take note:** Fully ripened bananas, the ones turning brown with some black spots, are the best for this recipe. They are much more flavorful and add moistness to the cookies.

1 Cookie: Calories 100; Total Fat 5g (Saturated Fat 2.5g; Trans Fat 0g); Cholesterol 10mg; Sodium 40mg; Total Carbohydrate 13g (Dietary Fiber 0g) **Exchanges:** 1 Other Carbohydrate, 1 Fat **Carbohydrate Choices:** 1

coconut macaroons

Prep Time: 40 Minutes
Start to Finish: 1 Hour 10 Minutes

About 2 dozen cookies

4 egg whites
⅔ cup sugar
¼ cup all-purpose flour
⅛ teaspoon salt
½ teaspoon almond extract
4 cups flaked coconut

1   Heat oven to 325°F. Spray cookie sheets with baking spray with flour, or line with cooking parchment paper. In large bowl, beat egg whites with electric mixer on high speed until foamy. Beat in sugar, flour, salt and almond extract until well blended. Stir in coconut.

2   On cookie sheets, drop dough by tablespoonfuls 2 inches apart.

3   Bake 13 to 17 minutes or until set and lightly browned. Immediately remove from cookie sheets to cooling racks. Cool completely, about 30 minutes. To keep macaroons moist and chewy, store between sheets of waxed paper or cooking parchment paper in a metal tin or plastic container with a tight-fitting lid.

High Altitude (3500–6500 ft): No change.

Holiday Coconut Macaroons: Stir in ¼ cup chopped red candied cherries and ¼ cup chopped green candied cherries with the coconut.

1 Cookie: Calories 100; Total Fat 5g (Saturated Fat 4.5g; Trans Fat 0g); Cholesterol 0mg; Sodium 60mg; Total Carbohydrate 13g (Dietary Fiber 0g) **Exchanges:** 1 Other Carbohydrate, 1 Fat **Carbohydrate Choices:** 1

pumpkin cookies with penuche frosting

Prep Time: 1 Hour
Start to Finish: 1 Hour

About 5 dozen cookies

COOKIES
½ cup granulated sugar
½ cup packed brown sugar
1 cup butter or margarine,
  softened
1 cup canned pumpkin (not
  pumpkin pie mix)
1 teaspoon vanilla
1 egg
2 cups all-purpose flour
1 teaspoon baking powder
1 teaspoon baking soda
1 teaspoon ground cinnamon
¼ teaspoon salt
¾ cup chopped nuts

FROSTING
3 tablespoons butter or
  margarine
½ cup packed brown sugar
¼ cup milk
1½ to 2 cups powdered sugar

1 Heat oven to 350°F. In large bowl, beat granulated sugar, ½ cup brown sugar and 1 cup butter with electric mixer on medium speed until light and fluffy. Beat in pumpkin, vanilla and egg until well blended. On low speed, beat in flour, baking powder, baking soda, cinnamon and salt until well blended. Stir in nuts.

2 On ungreased cookie sheets, drop dough by rounded teaspoonfuls 2 inches apart.

3 Bake 10 to 12 minutes or until light golden brown around edges. Immediately remove from cookie sheets to cooling racks. Cool completely, about 15 minutes.

4 Meanwhile, in 2-quart saucepan, heat 3 tablespoons butter and ½ cup brown sugar to boiling. Cook over medium heat about 1 minute, stirring constantly, until slightly thickened. Cool 10 minutes. Add milk; beat until smooth. Beat in enough powdered sugar until spreadable. Frost cookies.

High Altitude (3500–6500 ft): No change.

■■■ **take note:** Penuche ("pun-NOO-chee") is a fudgelike brown sugar candy and is derived from the Mexican word for "raw sugar" or "brown sugar." If the frosting becomes too stiff, stir in milk, 1 teaspoon at a time, or heat over low heat, stirring constantly.

1 Cookie: Calories 90; Total Fat 5g (Saturated Fat 2.5g; Trans Fat 0g); Cholesterol 15mg; Sodium 70mg; Total Carbohydrate 12g (Dietary Fiber 0g) **Exchanges:** ½ Starch, 1 Fat **Carbohydrate Choices:** 1

monster cookies

Prep Time: 1 Hour 15 Minutes
Start to Finish: 1 Hour 15 Minutes

About 4 dozen cookies

1 cup granulated sugar
1 cup packed brown sugar
1 cup peanut butter
½ cup butter or margarine,
  softened
3 eggs
4½ cups quick-cooking oats
2 teaspoons baking soda
1 cup semisweet chocolate chips
  (6 oz)
1 cup candy-coated chocolate
  candies
1 cup chopped peanuts
½ cup raisins

1 Heat oven to 350°F. In large bowl, beat granulated sugar, brown sugar, peanut butter and butter with electric mixer on medium speed until light and fluffy. Add eggs, one at a time, beating well after each addition. Beat in oats and baking soda. Stir in chocolate chips, chocolate candies, peanuts and raisins.

2 On ungreased cookie sheets, drop dough by heaping tablespoonfuls 2½ inches apart.

3 Bake 11 to 14 minutes or until light golden brown. Cool 2 minutes; remove from cookie sheets to cooling racks.

High Altitude (3500–6500 ft): Add ¼ cup water with the eggs; add ¼ cup all-purpose flour with the oats. Bake 13 to 16 minutes.

Monster Peanut Cookies: Substitute 1 cup candy-coated peanut butter candies for the candy-coated chocolate candies and 1 cup peanut butter chips for the chocolate chips.

▪▪▪ **take note:** These fun cookies, made with quick-cooking oats instead of wheat flour, are great for those who are gluten intolerant and can't eat wheat.

1 Cookie: Calories 180; Total Fat 9g (Saturated Fat 3.5g; Trans Fat 0g); Cholesterol 20mg; Sodium 110mg; Total Carbohydrate 22g (Dietary Fiber 1g) **Exchanges:** 1 Starch, ½ Other Carbohydrate, 1½ Fat **Carbohydrate Choices:** 1½

chunky chocolate cookies

Prep Time: 35 Minutes
Start to Finish: 50 Minutes

About 2 dozen cookies

>> 1 roll (16.5 oz) refrigerated sugar
cookies
3 tablespoons unsweetened
baking cocoa
1 cup semisweet chocolate
chunks
½ cup miniature semisweet
chocolate chips
½ cup chopped pecans

1 Heat oven to 350°F. In large bowl, break up cookie dough. Stir in cocoa, chocolate chunks, chocolate chips and pecans until well mixed.

2 On ungreased cookie sheets, drop dough by well-rounded tablespoonfuls 2 inches apart.

3 Bake 8 to 11 minutes or just until set. Cool 2 minutes; remove from cookie sheets to cooling racks. Cool completely, about 15 minutes.

High Altitude (3500–6500 ft): Bake 10 to 12 minutes.

Chunky Candy Cookies: Substitute ½ cup miniature candy-coated chocolate candies for the miniature chips and ½ cup chopped walnuts for the pecans.

1 Cookie: Calories 160; Total Fat 9g (Saturated Fat 3g; Trans Fat 1g); Cholesterol 5mg; Sodium 65mg; Total Carbohydrate 19g (Dietary Fiber 1g) **Exchanges:** ½ Starch, ½ Other Carbohydrate, 2 Fat **Carbohydrate Choices:** 1

chocolate chip cookies

Prep Time: 1 Hour 15 Minutes
Start to Finish: 1 Hour 15 Minutes

About 6 dozen cookies

1¼ cups granulated sugar
1¼ cups packed brown sugar
1½ cups butter or margarine,
   softened
2 teaspoons vanilla
3 eggs
4¼ cups all-purpose flour
2 teaspoons baking soda
½ teaspoon salt
1 bag (12 oz) semisweet
   chocolate chips (2 cups)

1 Heat oven to 375°F. In large bowl, beat granulated sugar, brown sugar and butter with electric mixer on medium speed until light and fluffy. Beat in vanilla and eggs until well blended. On low speed, beat in flour, baking soda and salt. Stir in chocolate chips.

2 On ungreased cookie sheets, drop dough by rounded tablespoonfuls 2 inches apart.

3 Bake 8 to 10 minutes or until light golden brown. Cool 1 minute; remove from cookie sheets to cooling racks.

High Altitude (3500–6500 ft): Bake 9 to 11 minutes.

Candy Cookies: Substitute 2 cups candy-coated chocolate candies for the chocolate chips.

■■■ **take note:** If you love lots of chocolate chips, stir in 2 bags (12 ounces each) chocolate chips instead of just 1 bag.

1 Cookie: Calories 120; Total Fat 6g (Saturated Fat 3.5g; Trans Fat 0g); Cholesterol 20mg; Sodium 85mg; Total Carbohydrate 16g (Dietary Fiber 0g) **Exchanges:** ½ Starch, ½ Other Carbohydrate, 1 Fat **Carbohydrate Choices:** 1

granola-apple cookies

Prep Time: 1 Hour 5 Minutes
Start to Finish: 1 Hour 20 Minutes

About 3 dozen cookies

COOKIES
1½ cups packed brown sugar
½ cup butter or margarine,
　softened
¼ cup milk
1 teaspoon grated lemon peel
1 tablespoon lemon juice
1 egg
1½ cups all-purpose flour
1 cup whole wheat flour
1 teaspoon baking soda
1 teaspoon ground cinnamon or
　nutmeg
¼ teaspoon salt
1½ cups finely chopped cooking
　apples
1 cup granola

GLAZE
¾ cup powdered sugar
2 to 3 teaspoons lemon juice

1 Heat oven to 375°F. In large bowl, beat brown sugar and butter with electric mixer on medium speed until light and fluffy. Beat in milk, lemon peel, 1 tablespoon lemon juice and the egg until well blended. On low speed, beat in all-purpose flour, whole wheat flour, baking soda, cinnamon and salt until well blended. Stir in apples and granola.

2 On ungreased cookie sheets, drop dough by heaping teaspoonfuls 2 inches apart.

3 Bake 9 to 13 minutes or until light golden brown. Immediately remove from cookie sheets to cooling racks. Cool completely, about 15 minutes.

4 In small bowl, mix glaze ingredients, adding enough lemon juice until glaze is smooth and thin enough to drizzle. Drizzle glaze over cookies.

High Altitude (3500–6500 ft): Decrease brown sugar to 1 cup.

■■■ **take note:** If you prefer, leave the peel on the apples for a little added fiber. Some good cooking apples for making these cookies are Cortland, Northern Spy, Rome Beauty, Winesap, Golden Delicious and Granny Smith. You may want to check your farmers' markets to see if there are local varieties that are good, too.

1 Cookie: Calories 120; Total Fat 3.5g (Saturated Fat 2g; Trans Fat 0g); Cholesterol 15mg; Sodium 75mg; Total Carbohydrate 21g (Dietary Fiber 1g) **Exchanges:** ½ Starch, 1 Other Carbohydrate, ½ Fat **Carbohydrate Choices:** 1½

oatmeal-raisin cookies

Prep Time: 1 Hour
Start to Finish: 1 Hour

About 3½ dozen cookies

¾ **cup granulated sugar**
¼ **cup packed brown sugar**
½ **cup butter or margarine,**
  softened
½ **teaspoon vanilla**
1 **egg**
¾ **cup all-purpose flour**
½ **teaspoon baking soda**
½ **teaspoon ground cinnamon**
¼ **teaspoon salt**
1½ **cups quick-cooking or old-**
  fashioned oats
½ **cup raisins**
½ **cup chopped nuts**

1 Heat oven to 375°F. Spray cookie sheets with cooking spray.

2 In large bowl, beat granulated sugar, brown sugar and butter with electric mixer on medium speed until light and fluffy. Beat in vanilla and egg until well blended. On low speed, beat in flour, baking soda, cinnamon and salt. Stir in oats, raisins and nuts.

3 On cookie sheets, drop dough by rounded teaspoonfuls 2 inches apart.

4 Bake 7 to 10 minutes or until edges are light golden brown. Cool 1 minute; remove from cookie sheets to cooling racks.

High Altitude (3500–6500 ft): Increase flour to 1 cup.

Oatmeal-Cranberry Cookies: Substitute ½ cup sweetened dried cranberries for the raisins.

■■■ **take note:** These cookies are great for lunch bags or to have on hand for a "grab and go" treat. Freeze 1 or 2 cookies each in small resealable plastic freezer bags. Place the individual bags in an airtight container and freeze up to 6 months.

1 Cookie: Calories 80; Total Fat 3.5g (Saturated Fat 1.5g; Trans Fat 0g); Cholesterol 10mg; Sodium 45mg; Total Carbohydrate 10g (Dietary Fiber 0g) **Exchanges:** ½ Starch, 1 Fat **Carbohydrate Choices:** ½

dulce de leche cookies

Prep Time: 1 Hour 15 Minutes
Start to Finish: 1 Hour 45 Minutes

About 40 sandwich cookies

GARNISH
1 cup flaked coconut

COOKIES
1 cup butter or margarine,
    softened
2/3 cup sugar
2 egg yolks
3 tablespoons dark rum or
    1/2 teaspoon rum extract plus
    2 1/2 tablespoons water
1 teaspoon vanilla
2 1/2 cups all-purpose flour
1 teaspoon baking powder
1/4 teaspoon salt
1/4 cup sugar

FILLING
1 cup caramel apple dip
    (from 16-oz container)

1. Heat oven to 350°F. Spread coconut in ungreased shallow pan. Bake uncovered 5 to 7 minutes, stirring occasionally, until golden brown. Set aside.

2. In large bowl, beat butter and 2/3 cup sugar with electric mixer on medium speed about 1 minute or until smooth. Add egg yolks, rum and vanilla. Beat on high speed about 1 minute or until blended.

3. In medium bowl, stir together flour, baking powder and salt. Stir flour mixture into butter mixture until well blended. Cover; refrigerate 30 minutes.

4. Spray cookie sheets with cooking spray. Shape dough into 3/4-inch balls; place about 2 inches apart on cookie sheets. Dip bottom of small glass into 1/4 cup sugar; press on cookies to make about 1 1/2 inches in diameter.

5. Bake 10 to 11 minutes or just until edges begin to brown. Remove from cookie sheets to cooling racks. Cool completely, about 15 minutes.

6. For each sandwich cookie, spread about 1 teaspoon of the caramel apple dip on bottom of 1 cookie, spreading to edge of cookie. Top with second cookie. Gently squeeze until filling oozes out a little around the side. Roll edges of cookies in toasted coconut.

High Altitude (3500–6500 ft): No change.

■■■ **take note:** You can use a dulce de leche (caramelized sweetened condensed milk) instead of the caramel apple dip. Look for it in the Hispanic-foods section of your supermarket.

1 Sandwich Cookie: Calories 120; Total Fat 6g (Saturated Fat 3.5g; Trans Fat 0g); Cholesterol 25mg; Sodium 95mg; Total Carbohydrate 17g (Dietary Fiber 0g) **Exchanges:** 1/2 Starch, 1/2 Other Carbohydrate, 1 Fat **Carbohydrate Choices:** 1

chocolate chip–cranberry-pecan cookies

Prep Time: 40 Minutes
Start to Finish: 1 Hour 20 Minutes

About 2 dozen cookies

>> **1 roll (16.5 oz) refrigerated
chocolate chip cookies**
**½ cup sweetened dried
cranberries**
¼ cup chopped pecans
½ cup vanilla baking chips
1 teaspoon vegetable oil

1 Heat oven to 350°F. In large bowl, break up cookie dough. Stir or knead in cranberries and pecans. Work with half of dough at a time; refrigerate remaining dough until needed.

2 On ungreased cookie sheets, drop dough by well-rounded tablespoonfuls 2 inches apart. Repeat with remaining dough.

3 Bake 9 to 13 minutes or until light golden brown. Cool 1 minute; remove from cookie sheets to cooling racks. Cool completely, about 15 minutes.

4 In small resealable freezer plastic bag, place vanilla baking chips and oil; seal bag. Microwave on High 30 seconds or until chunks are softened. If necessary, microwave 10 to 15 seconds longer. Squeeze bag until mixture is smooth.

5 Cut ⅛-inch tip from one bottom corner of bag. Squeeze bag gently to drizzle white chocolate over cookies. Let stand about 40 minutes or until chocolate is set.

High Altitude (3500–6500 ft): Bake 10 to 13 minutes.

Chocolate Chip–Cherry-Macadamia Cookies: Substitute ½ cup dried cherries for the cranberries and ¼ cup chopped macadamia nuts for the pecans.

1 Cookie: Calories 140; Total Fat 7g (Saturated Fat 2.5g; Trans Fat 1g); Cholesterol 0mg; Sodium 65mg; Total Carbohydrate 17g (Dietary Fiber 1g) **Exchanges:** ½ Starch, ½ Other Carbohydrate, 1½ Fat **Carbohydrate Choices:** 1

chocolate-dipped almond-toffee moons

Prep Time: 2 Hours
Start to Finish: 2 Hours

About 5 dozen cookies

COOKIES
½ cup powdered sugar
1 cup butter or margarine, softened
2 teaspoons vanilla
2 cups all-purpose flour
1 cup finely chopped or ground almonds
¼ teaspoon salt
½ cup toffee bits

GLAZE
½ cup semisweet chocolate chips
2 teaspoons shortening
Additional toffee bits, if desired

1 Heat oven to 325°F. In large bowl, beat powdered sugar, butter and vanilla with electric mixer on medium speed until light and fluffy. On low speed, beat in flour, almonds and salt until well blended. Stir in ½ cup toffee bits.

2 Shape dough into 1-inch balls. Shape each ball into 2-inch-long log; bend into crescent shape. On ungreased cookie sheets, place crescents 1 inch apart.

3 Bake 13 to 15 minutes or until set and bottoms are golden brown. Immediately remove from cookie sheets to cooling racks. Cool completely, about 30 minutes.

4 In 1-cup microwavable measuring cup, microwave chocolate chips and shortening on High 30 seconds. Stir; continue microwaving, stirring every 10 seconds, until chocolate is melted and can be stirred smooth. Dip 1 end of each cookie halfway into melted chocolate, letting excess drip off. If desired, sprinkle additional toffee bits over chocolate. Place on waxed paper or cooking parchment paper until set.

High Altitude (3500–6500 ft): No change.

Chocolate-Dipped Pecan-Toffee Moons: Substitute 1 cup finely chopped or ground pecans for the almonds.

■■■ **take note:** To grind nuts in the food processor, pulse the nuts with a spoonful of sugar just until they are ground. The sugar helps keep the nuts dry. Take care not to overprocess them or they will become oily.

1 Cookie: Calories 80; Total Fat 5g (Saturated Fat 2.5g; Trans Fat 0g); Cholesterol 10mg; Sodium 40mg; Total Carbohydrate 6g (Dietary Fiber 0g) **Exchanges:** ½ Starch, 1 Fat **Carbohydrate Choices:** ½

mint-kissed meringues

Prep Time: 20 Minutes
Start to Finish: 2 Hours 25 Minutes

About 4 dozen cookies

2 egg whites
¼ teaspoon cream of tartar
⅛ teaspoon salt
½ cup sugar
¼ teaspoon mint extract
3 to 5 drops green food color
Multicolored candy sprinkles,
   if desired

1 Heat oven to 200°F. Spray 2 large cookie sheets with cooking spray.

2 In small bowl, beat egg whites, cream of tartar and salt with electric mixer on medium speed until foamy. On high speed, add sugar, 1 tablespoon at a time, beating until sugar is dissolved, meringue is glossy and very stiff peaks form. Beat in mint extract. With rubber spatula, fold in food color, 1 drop at a time, until well blended and desired color.

3 To shape cookies, use disposable decorating bag or gallon-size food-storage plastic bag with ½-inch hole cut in one bottom corner of bag (if desired, fit large star tip in decorating bag or in hole of plastic bag). Spoon meringue into bag; twist top of bag to seal. Squeeze bag to pipe meringue into 1-inch puffs onto cookie sheets. Sprinkle each with candy sprinkles.

4 Bake on middle oven rack 2 hours. Immediately remove cookies from cookie sheets to cooling racks. Cool completely, about 5 minutes. Meringue becomes tough if it absorbs moisture; store in a loosely covered container at room temperature. If the humidity is high, transfer them to a tightly covered container.

High Altitude (3500–6500 ft): When making meringue, beat until sugar is dissolved, meringue is glossy and soft peaks form.

Chocolate Chip–Kissed Meringues: Omit food color. Stir 1 cup miniature chocolate chips into the meringue before piping it onto the cookie sheet.

1 Cookie: Calories 10; Total Fat 0g (Saturated Fat 0g; Trans Fat 0g); Cholesterol 0mg; Sodium 10mg; Total Carbohydrate 2g (Dietary Fiber 0g) **Exchanges:** Free **Carbohydrate Choices:** 0

gingersnaps

Prep Time: 1 Hour 15 Minutes
Start to Finish: 2 Hours 15 Minutes

About 5 dozen cookies

1 cup sugar
¾ cup butter or margarine,
    softened
¼ cup molasses
1 egg
2¼ cups all-purpose flour
2 teaspoons baking soda
1 teaspoon ground cinnamon
½ teaspoon salt
½ teaspoon ground ginger
½ teaspoon ground cloves
¼ teaspoon ground nutmeg
¼ cup sugar

1 In large bowl, beat 1 cup sugar, the butter, molasses and egg with electric mixer on medium speed until light and fluffy. On low speed, beat in remaining ingredients except ¼ cup sugar until well blended. Cover with plastic wrap; refrigerate 1 hour for easier handling.

2 Heat oven to 350°F. Shape dough into 1-inch balls; roll in ¼ cup sugar. On ungreased cookie sheets, place balls 2 inches apart.

3 Bake 8 to 12 minutes or until set. (Cookies will puff up, then flatten during baking.) Cool 1 minute; remove from cookie sheets to cooling racks.

High Altitude (3500–6500 ft): Decrease baking soda to 1½ teaspoons.

Chocolate Star Gingersnaps: Immediately after cookies are removed from the oven, press a chocolate star candy in center of each cookie. Cool 1 minute; remove from cookie sheets to cooling rack.

1 Cookie: Calories 60; Total Fat 2.5g (Saturated Fat 1.5g; Trans Fat 0g); Cholesterol 10mg; Sodium 80mg; Total Carbohydrate 9g (Dietary Fiber 0g) **Exchanges:** ½ Other Carbohydrate, ½ Fat **Carbohydrate Choices:** ½

no-roll sugar cookies

Prep Time: 1 Hour 20 Minutes
Start to Finish: 3 Hours 20 Minutes

About 10 dozen cookies

1 cup granulated sugar
1 cup powdered sugar
1 cup butter or margarine, softened
1 cup vegetable oil
1 teaspoon vanilla
2 eggs
4¼ cups all-purpose flour
1 teaspoon baking soda
1 teaspoon cream of tartar
1 teaspoon salt
About ⅓ cup colored or granulated sugar

1 In large bowl, beat granulated sugar, powdered sugar and butter with electric mixer on medium speed until light and fluffy. Beat in oil, vanilla and eggs until well blended. On low speed, beat in flour, baking soda, cream of tartar and salt until dough forms. Cover with plastic wrap; refrigerate at least 2 hours for easier handling.

2 Heat oven to 375°F. Shape dough into 1-inch balls. On ungreased cookie sheets, place balls 2 inches apart. Slightly flatten one of the balls with the bottom of small glass before dipping into colored sugar so the sugar sticks to the glass. Using bottom of glass dipped in colored sugar, flatten each ball to ¼-inch thickness.

3 Bake 5 to 8 minutes or until set but not brown. Immediately remove from cookie sheets to cooling racks.

High Altitude (3500–6500 ft): Bake 6 to 7 minutes.

■■■ **take note:** For the prettiest cookies, press the dough with a "cut-glass" tumbler with a pretty design on the bottom. Or use a fork dipped in colored sugar to make a crisscross design.

1 Cookie: Calories 60; Total Fat 3.5g (Saturated Fat 1.5g; Trans Fat 0g); Cholesterol 10mg; Sodium 40mg; Total Carbohydrate 7g (Dietary Fiber 0g) **Exchanges:** ½ Other Carbohydrate, ½ Fat **Carbohydrate Choices:** ½

mexican wedding cakes

Prep Time: 1 Hour 30 Minutes
Start to Finish: 1 Hour 30 Minutes

About 4½ dozen cookies

½ cup powdered sugar
1 cup butter or margarine,
    softened
2 teaspoons vanilla
2 cups all-purpose flour
1 cup finely chopped or ground
    almonds or pecans
¼ teaspoon salt
¾ cup powdered sugar

1   Heat oven to 325°F. In large bowl, beat ½ cup powdered sugar, the butter and vanilla with electric mixer on medium speed until light and fluffy. On low speed, beat in flour, almonds and salt until dough forms.

2   Shape dough into 1-inch balls. On ungreased cookie sheets, place balls 1 inch apart.

3   Bake 13 to 17 minutes or until set but not brown. Immediately remove from cookie sheets to cooling racks. Cool slightly, about 10 minutes.

4   Place ¾ cup powdered sugar in small bowl. Roll cookies in powdered sugar. Cool completely, about 15 minutes. Roll in powdered sugar again. Cookies can be placed in an airtight container and freeze up to 3 weeks. Before serving, thaw the cookies and reroll them in powdered sugar.

High Altitude (3500–6500 ft): No change.

take note: These rich butter cookies are also known as Russian Tea Cakes, Swedish Tea Cakes and Greek Wedding Cookies.

1 Cookie: Calories 70; Total Fat 4.5g (Saturated Fat 2.5g; Trans Fat 0g); Cholesterol 10mg; Sodium 35mg; Total Carbohydrate 7g (Dietary Fiber 0g) **Exchanges:** ½ Other Carbohydrate, 1 Fat **Carbohydrate Choices:** ½

Kid Kookies

You'll need purchased peanut-shaped sandwich cookies with peanut butter filling and chocolate- or vanilla-flavored candy coating. Dip cookies in coating and let excess drip off. Place on a waxed paper– or cooking parchment paper–lined cookie sheet and decorate. Let stand about 15 minutes until set.

Cutie Bugs: Cut pretzels into curved pieces for legs and shorter pieces for antennae. Dip one end in coating; place three legs on each side and two short pieces on top of each cookie. Add mini candy-coated chocolate baking bits for eyes.

Snow Kids: Add mini chocolate chips for eyes. Decorate with strips of fruit snack roll and candies.

Peanutty Ghost: Add mini chocolate chips for eyes and mouth. Or use black decorating gel to make O-shaped mouth, if desired.

orange shortbread bites

Prep Time: 1 Hour
Start to Finish: 1 Hour

100 squares

1 cup butter or margarine,
   softened
½ cup powdered sugar
2 cups all-purpose flour
1 tablespoon grated orange peel
¼ cup miniature semisweet
   chocolate chips
2 oz white chocolate baking bar,
   chopped
Candy sprinkles or small candy
   decors, if desired

1 Heat oven to 325°F. In large bowl, beat butter and powdered sugar with electric mixer on medium speed about 1 minute or until fluffy. On low speed, beat in flour and orange peel until well blended. Stir in chocolate chips.

2 On work surface, pat dough into 6½×6½-inch square, ¾ inch thick. With floured knife, cut 10 rows by 10 rows. On ungreased cookie sheets, place squares ½ inch apart.

3 Bake 18 to 22 minutes or until firm to the touch and set. Remove from cookie sheets to cooling racks. Cool completely, about 10 minutes.

4 In small microwavable bowl, microwave white chocolate on High 30 seconds; stir. If necessary, microwave in 10-second increments, stirring after each time, until smooth. Spread white chocolate over top of each cookie. If using candy sprinkles, frost just a few cookies at a time, then add the candy sprinkles because the white chocolate sets up quickly.

High Altitude (3500–6500 ft): No change.

■■■ **take note:** Instead of frosting with melted white chocolate, you can roll the warm cookies in powdered sugar to coat them.

1 Cookie: Calories 35; Total Fat 2.5g (Saturated Fat 1.5g; Trans Fat 0g); Cholesterol 5mg; Sodium 15mg; Total Carbohydrate 3g (Dietary Fiber 0g) **Exchanges:** ½ Fat **Carbohydrate Choices:** 0

peanut butter cookies

Prep Time: 1 Hour
Start to Finish: 1 Hour

About 4 dozen cookies

½ cup granulated sugar
½ cup packed brown sugar
½ cup butter or margarine, softened
½ cup peanut butter
1 teaspoon vanilla
1 egg
1¼ cups all-purpose flour
1 teaspoon baking soda
½ teaspoon salt
4 teaspoons granulated sugar

1 Heat oven to 375°F. In large bowl, beat ½ cup granulated sugar, the brown sugar and butter with electric mixer on medium speed until light and fluffy. Beat in peanut butter, vanilla and egg until well blended. On low speed, beat in flour, baking soda and salt.

2 Shape dough into 1-inch balls. On ungreased cookie sheets, place balls 2 inches apart. With fork dipped in 4 teaspoons granulated sugar, flatten balls in crisscross pattern.

3 Bake 6 to 9 minutes or until set and golden brown. Immediately remove from cookie sheets to cooling racks.

High Altitude (3500–6500 ft): Increase flour to 1½ cups.

Chocolate Chip–Peanut Butter Cookies: Stir in 1 cup (6 oz) semisweet chocolate chips with the flour.

Peanut Butter–Candy Cookies: Omit 4 teaspoons granulated sugar. Stir in 1 cup candy-coated chocolate candies with the flour.

Nutty Peanut Butter Cookies: Stir in 1 cup chopped peanuts with the flour.

1 Cookie: Calories 70; Total Fat 3.5g (Saturated Fat 1.5g; Trans Fat 0g); Cholesterol 10mg; Sodium 80mg; Total Carbohydrate 8g (Dietary Fiber 0g) **Exchanges:** ½ Starch, ½ Fat **Carbohydrate Choices:** ½

iced lemon cookies

Prep Time: 1 Hour 20 Minutes
Start to Finish: 3 Hours 20 Minutes

About 5 dozen cookies

COOKIES
½ cup butter or margarine, softened
½ cup granulated sugar
½ cup powdered sugar
1 egg
½ cup vegetable oil
1 teaspoon grated lemon peel
2¼ cups all-purpose flour
½ teaspoon baking soda
½ teaspoon cream of tartar
¼ teaspoon salt
3 tablespoons granulated sugar

TOPPING
2 cups powdered sugar
3 to 4 tablespoons fresh lemon juice
¾ cup coarsely chopped pistachio nuts

1 In large bowl, beat butter, ½ cup granulated sugar and ½ cup powdered sugar with electric mixer on medium speed until light and fluffy. Beat in egg, oil and lemon peel until well blended. On low speed, beat in flour, baking soda, cream of tartar and salt until well blended. Cover with plastic wrap; refrigerate 2 hours for easier handling.

2 Heat oven to 325°F. Shape dough into 1-inch balls. On ungreased cookie sheets, place balls 2 inches apart. Dip bottom of small glass into 3 tablespoons sugar; press on cookies to make about 2 inches in diameter.

3 Bake 9 to 11 minutes or until edges begin to set and cookies are light golden brown. Cool 2 minutes; remove from cookie sheets to cooling racks. Cool completely, about 10 minutes.

4 Meanwhile, in small bowl, mix 2 cups powdered sugar and enough lemon juice until smooth and spreadable. Spread frosting on cookies. Sprinkle nuts on frosting before it sets.

High Altitude (3500–6500 ft): No change.

Iced Lime Cookies: Substitute 1 teaspoon grated lime peel for the lemon peel and 3 to 4 tablespoons fresh lime juice for the lemon juice.

■■■ **take note:** When the pale green pistachio nut matures, its hard, buff-colored shell splits open. Pistachios are sold in their natural color or dyed red. Use either color to garnish these lemon cookies.

1 Cookie: Calories 90; Total Fat 4g (Saturated Fat 1.5g; Trans Fat 0g); Cholesterol 10mg; Sodium 35mg; Total Carbohydrate 11g (Dietary Fiber 0g) **Exchanges:** 1 Other Carbohydrate, 1 Fat **Carbohydrate Choices:** 1

snickerdoodles

Prep Time: 1 Hour
Start to Finish: 1 Hour

About 4 dozen cookies

1½ cups sugar
½ cup butter or margarine,
  softened
1 teaspoon vanilla
2 eggs
2¾ cups all-purpose flour
1 teaspoon cream of tartar
½ teaspoon baking soda
¼ teaspoon salt
2 tablespoons sugar
2 teaspoons ground cinnamon

1 Cookie: Calories 70; Total Fat 2g (Saturated Fat 1.5g; Trans Fat 0g); Cholesterol 15mg; Sodium 40mg; Total Carbohydrate 12g (Dietary Fiber 0g) **Exchanges:** 1 Other Carbohydrate, ½ Fat **Carbohydrate Choices:** 1

1 Heat oven to 400°F. In large bowl, beat 1½ cups sugar and the butter with electric mixer on medium speed until light and fluffy. Beat in vanilla and eggs until well blended. On low speed, beat in flour, cream of tartar, baking soda and salt until well blended.

2 In small bowl, mix 2 tablespoons sugar and the cinnamon. Shape dough into 1-inch balls; roll in sugar-cinnamon mixture and place 2 inches apart on ungreased cookie sheets.

3 Bake 8 to 10 minutes or until set. Immediately remove from cookie sheets to cooling racks.

High Altitude (3500–6500 ft): Bake 7 to 9 minutes.

Chocolate Snickerdoodles: Substitute ½ cup unsweetened baking cocoa for ½ cup of the flour. Bake 6 to 9 minutes.

Whole Wheat Snickerdoodles: Substitute 1 cup whole wheat flour and 1 cup all-purpose flour for the 2¾ cups all-purpose flour. Bake at 350°F for 10 to 14 minutes or until set.

more family favorites

sugar-and-spice shortbread sticks

Prep Time: 1 Hour
Start to Finish: 2 Hours

About 4 dozen cookies

COOKIES
¾ cup packed brown sugar
1 cup butter or margarine,
   softened
1 teaspoon vanilla
1 egg
2¾ cups all-purpose flour
¾ teaspoon apple pie spice

GLAZE
1½ cups powdered sugar
½ teaspoon apple pie spice
1 to 2 tablespoons apple juice or
   water

1 In large bowl, beat brown sugar, butter, vanilla and egg with electric mixer on medium speed until light and fluffy. On low speed, beat in flour and ¾ teaspoon apple pie spice until well blended. Divide dough in half; shape each half into flattened disk. Wrap each in plastic wrap; refrigerate about 1 hour for easier handling.

2 Heat oven to 350°F. On lightly floured surface, roll half of dough at a time to 12×6-inch rectangle, using lightly floured rolling pin. (Keep remaining half of dough refrigerated.) Cut dough rectangle in half lengthwise; cut each half crosswise into 1-inch-wide sticks. On ungreased cookie sheets, place sticks ½ inch apart.

3 Bake 12 to 15 minutes or until edges are light golden brown. Immediately remove from cookie sheets to cooling racks. Cool completely, about 10 minutes.

4 Meanwhile, in small bowl, stir glaze ingredients until smooth, adding enough apple juice until glaze is spreadable. Spread glaze on tops of cookies. Let stand until glaze is set before storing.

High Altitude (3500–6500 ft): No change.

take note: If you don't have apple pie spice, use ½ teaspoon ground cinnamon, ⅛ teaspoon each ground cloves and ground allspice, plus a pinch of ground nutmeg.

1 Cookie: Calories 90; Total Fat 4g (Saturated Fat 2.5g; Trans Fat 0g); Cholesterol 15mg; Sodium 30mg; Total Carbohydrate 13g (Dietary Fiber 0g) **Exchanges:** ½ Starch, ½ Other Carbohydrate, ½ Fat **Carbohydrate Choices:** 1

`easy` secret-center cookie cups

Prep Time: 1 Hour 10 Minutes
Start to Finish: 1 Hour 10 Minutes

About 3 dozen cookies

>> **1 roll (16.5 oz) refrigerated peanut butter cookies**

36 miniature (about 1-inch square) milk chocolate-covered peanut, caramel and nougat candy bars, unwrapped

36 small (1¾-inch) paper baking cups

1 container (1 lb) chocolate ready-to-spread frosting

1 Heat oven to 375°F. For each cookie cup, wrap 1 heaping teaspoonful of cookie dough around 1 candy bar, enclosing it almost completely and forming ball. Place in paper baking cup. On ungreased cookie sheets, place cups 1 inch apart.

2 Bake 8 to 12 minutes or until golden brown. Centers of cookies will sink slightly. Cool 1 minute; remove from cookie sheets to cooling racks. Cool completely, about 15 minutes.

3 Spoon frosting into decorating bag fitted with a star tip. Pipe frosting on top of each cookie cup. Or use a spoon and add a dollop of frosting to the top of each cookie cup.

High Altitude (3500–6500 ft): No change.

■■■ **take note:** These little cups can be filled with almost any "secret" center. Use different miniature candy bars or chocolate candies for a different center each time.

1 Cookie: Calories 160; Total Fat 8g (Saturated Fat 4g; Trans Fat 0g); Cholesterol 0mg; Sodium 80mg; Total Carbohydrate 21g (Dietary Fiber 0g) **Exchanges:** ½ Starch, 1 Other Carbohydrate, 1½ Fat **Carbohydrate Choices:** 1½

s'more thumbprint cookies

Prep Time: 1 Hour
Start to Finish: 1 Hour

5 dozen cookies

1 cup butter or margarine,
   softened
½ cup packed brown sugar
1 egg
1 teaspoon vanilla
1⅓ cups all-purpose flour
1 cup finely ground or crushed
   graham cracker crumbs
   (16 cracker squares)
⅛ teaspoon salt
120 miniature marshmallows
   (about 1¼ cups) or 30 regular
   marshmallows, cut into
   quarters
60 rectangles milk chocolate
   candy (from four 1.55-oz bars)

1   Heat oven to 325°F. In large bowl, beat butter and brown sugar with electric mixer on medium speed until light and fluffy. Beat in egg and vanilla until well blended. Add flour, cracker crumbs and salt; on low speed, beat about 1 minute or until stiff dough forms.

2   Shape dough by heaping teaspoonfuls into 60 balls. On ungreased cookie sheets, place balls 2 inches apart. With thumb, make indentation in center of each.

3   Bake 10 to 12 minutes or until cookies are firm and edges are just beginning to brown. Lightly press 2 marshmallows in center of each cookie; bake 2 to 3 minutes longer.

4   Top marshmallows on each cookie with 1 rectangle of chocolate; let stand 2 to 3 minutes. With tip of knife, gently spread chocolate over marshmallows. Let stand until chocolate is set.

High Altitude (3500–6500 ft): Increase flour to 2 cups. Bake 12 to 14 minutes.

■■■ **take note:** To make ground graham cracker crumbs, break the graham cracker squares into a food processor bowl with a metal blade. Cover and process until fine crumbs. Or place graham crackers in a resealable food-storage plastic bag and press with a rolling pin or bottle until very finely crushed.

1 Cookie: Calories 70; Total Fat 4g (Saturated Fat 2.5g; Trans Fat 0g); Cholesterol 10mg; Sodium 40mg; Total Carbohydrate 8g (Dietary Fiber 0g) **Exchanges:** ½ Other Carbohydrate, 1 Fat **Carbohydrate Choices:** ½

butterscotch-pecan cookie wedges

Prep Time: 30 Minutes
Start to Finish: 1 Hour 50 Minutes

About 32 wedges

>> 1 roll (16.5 oz) refrigerated sugar cookies
1 box (4-serving size) butterscotch instant pudding and pie filling mix
2 tablespoons milk
1 cup chopped pecans
½ cup semisweet chocolate chips
1 teaspoon vegetable oil

1 Heat oven to 350°F. In large bowl, break up cookie dough. Stir in pudding mix and milk until well blended. Stir or knead in ½ cup of the pecans. Shape dough into flattened round. Cover; refrigerate about 30 minutes or until slightly firm.

2 Divide dough into 4 pieces. On ungreased large cookie sheet, press each piece into 6-inch round.

3 Bake 13 to 17 minutes or until edges are golden brown. Immediately cut each round into 8 wedges. Remove from cookie sheet to cooling rack. Cool completely, about 30 minutes.

4 In 1-quart saucepan, heat chocolate chips and oil over low heat about 2 minutes, stirring constantly, until chips are melted and smooth. Dip one cut side of each wedge into melted chocolate mixture; immediately sprinkle with remaining ½ cup pecans. Place on waxed paper or cooking parchment paper until set.

High Altitude (3500–6500 ft): Bake 13 to 15 minutes.

■■■ **take note:** You can melt the chocolate chips in the microwave. Place the chips and oil in a small microwavable bowl. Microwave on High for 30 seconds. Stir; continue microwaving, stirring every 10 seconds, until chocolate is melted and can be stirred smooth.

1 Wedge: Calories 120; Total Fat 6g (Saturated Fat 1.5g; Trans Fat 1g); Cholesterol 5mg; Sodium 95mg; Total Carbohydrate 14g (Dietary Fiber 0g) **Exchanges:** ½ Starch, ½ Other Carbohydrate, 1 Fat **Carbohydrate Choices:** 1

chocolate chip–raspberry jam strips

Prep Time: 1 Hour 15 Minutes
Start to Finish: 1 Hour 30 Minutes

4 dozen cookies

COOKIES
⅔ cup butter or margarine,
   softened
⅓ cup sugar
1 teaspoon almond extract
1 egg
2 cups all-purpose flour
½ teaspoon baking powder
½ cup miniature semisweet
   chocolate chips
½ cup seedless raspberry jam

ICING
⅓ cup miniature semisweet
   chocolate chips
1 teaspoon shortening

1   Heat oven to 350°F. In large bowl, beat butter and sugar with electric mixer on medium speed until light and fluffy. Beat in almond extract and egg until well blended. On low speed, beat in flour and baking powder until well blended. Stir in ½ cup chocolate chips.

2   Divide dough into 4 equal parts. On lightly floured surface, shape each part into 12-inch log. On 2 ungreased cookie sheets, place logs about 3 inches apart. Using handle of wooden spoon or finger, make depression about ½ inch wide and ¼ inch deep lengthwise down center of each log. Stir the jam; fill each roll with 2 tablespoons jam.

3   Bake 15 to 20 minutes or until light golden brown. Cool 5 minutes. Cut each baked log diagonally into 12 cookies; place on cooling racks. Cool completely, about 10 minutes.

4   Meanwhile, in small microwavable bowl, microwave icing ingredients on High 30 seconds. Stir; continue microwaving, stirring every 10 seconds, until chocolate is melted and can be stirred smooth. Drizzle icing over cookies. Let stand until icing is set before storing. Store in loosely covered container.

High Altitude (3500–6500 ft): Bake 17 to 22 minutes.

Chocolate Chip–Apricot Jam Strips: Substitute ½ cup apricot preserves for the raspberry jam.

Chocolate Chip–Strawberry Jam Strips: Substitute 1 teaspoon vanilla for the almond extract and ½ cup strawberry preserves for the raspberry jam.

■■■ **take note:** You can use raspberry jam with seeds, but the seedless jam is prettier because it is more bright and clear.

1 Cookie: Calories 70; Total Fat 3.5g (Saturated Fat 2g; Trans Fat 0g); Cholesterol 10mg; Sodium 25mg; Total Carbohydrate 10g (Dietary Fiber 0g) **Exchanges:** 1 Other Carbohydrate, ½ Fat **Carbohydrate Choices:** ½

date pinwheel cookies

Prep Time: 1 Hour
Start to Finish: 4 Hours

About 5 dozen cookies

COOKIES
1 cup packed brown sugar
½ cup butter or margarine,
    softened
1 egg
1½ cups all-purpose flour
1½ teaspoons baking powder
¼ teaspoon salt

FILLING
¾ cup finely chopped dates
¼ cup granulated sugar
⅓ cup water
2 tablespoons finely chopped
    nuts

1 In large bowl, beat brown sugar, butter and egg with electric mixer on medium speed until light and fluffy. On low speed, beat in flour, baking powder and salt until dough forms. Cover with plastic wrap; refrigerate 1 hour for easier handling.

2 Meanwhile, in 1-quart saucepan, heat dates, granulated sugar and water to boiling. Reduce heat to low. Cover; simmer about 5 minutes or until thick. Stir in nuts. Cool 15 minutes.

3 On lightly floured surface, roll dough into 16×8-inch rectangle, using lightly floured rolling pin. Carefully spread date filling over dough. Roll up dough jelly-roll fashion, starting at 16-inch side; cut in half to form two 8-inch rolls. Wrap each roll in plastic wrap; refrigerate 2 hours or until firm.

4 Heat oven to 375°F. Cut dough into ¼-inch slices. On ungreased cookie sheets, place slices 2 inches apart.

5 Bake 6 to 9 minutes or until light golden brown. Immediately remove from cookie sheets to cooling racks.

High Altitude (3500–6500 ft): Increase flour to 1½ cups plus 2 tablespoons.

Apricot Pinwheel Cookies: Substitute ¾ cup finely chopped dried apricots for the dates.

Fig Pinwheel Cookies: Substitute ¾ cup finely chopped dried figs for the dates.

Orange-Spice Date Pinwheel Cookies: Add ½ teaspoon grated orange peel and 1 teaspoon ground cinnamon to the cookie dough.

1 Cookie: Calories 50; Total Fat 2g (Saturated Fat 1g; Trans Fat 0g); Cholesterol 10mg; Sodium 35mg; Total Carbohydrate 9g (Dietary Fiber 0g) **Exchanges:** ½ Other Carbohydrate, ½ Fat **Carbohydrate Choices:** ½

date-filled cookies

Prep Time: 1 Hour
Start to Finish: 3 Hours

About 3½ dozen cookies

COOKIES
1½ cups packed brown sugar
1 cup butter or margarine,
    softened
1 teaspoon vanilla
3 eggs
3½ cups all-purpose flour
1 teaspoon baking soda

FILLING
2 cups chopped dates
1 cup granulated sugar
1 cup water

1 In large bowl, beat brown sugar and butter with electric mixer on medium speed until light and fluffy. Beat in vanilla and eggs until well blended. On low speed, beat in flour and baking soda until well blended. Cover with plastic wrap; refrigerate at least 2 hours for easier handling.

2 Meanwhile, in 2-quart saucepan, heat filling ingredients to boiling, stirring frequently. Reduce heat to low; simmer 10 minutes, stirring frequently. Refrigerate until ready to use. (Mixture will thicken as it cools.)

3 Heat oven to 375°F. On well-floured surface, roll ⅓ of dough at a time to ⅛-inch thickness, using lightly floured rolling pin. (Keep remaining dough refrigerated.) Cut with floured 2½-inch round cookie cutter. In half of cookies, cut and remove 1-inch round or desired shape hole from center. Place whole cookies on ungreased cookie sheets. Spoon 1 teaspoon cooled filling onto center of each. Top each with dough ring. Using fingertips or fork, press edges of dough to seal. Return dough centers to remaining dough for rerolling.

4 Bake 7 to 10 minutes or until light golden brown. Cool 1 minute; remove from cookie sheets to cooling racks.

High Altitude (3500–6500 ft): No change.

Fig-Filled Cookies: Substitute 2 cups chopped dried figs for the dates.

Orange Date-Filled Cookies: In the filling, substitute 1 cup orange juice for the water. Add ¼ cup finely chopped walnuts with the dates.

1 Cookie: Calories 160; Total Fat 5g (Saturated Fat 3g; Trans Fat 0g); Cholesterol 25mg; Sodium 70mg; Total Carbohydrate 27g (Dietary Fiber 1g) **Exchanges:** 2 Other Carbohydrate, 1 Fat **Carbohydrate Choices:** 2

(top left) Raspberry-Filled Brownie Delights, page 52; *(top right)* Apricot-Caramel-Coconut Bars, page 74; *(bottom)* Caramel Chai Bars, page 84

CHAPTER TWO

Bake-Off® winners

white chocolate chunk cookies

Dottie Due | Edgewood, KY | Bake-Off® Contest 33, 1988

Prep Time: 1 Hour 30 Minutes
Start to Finish: 1 Hour 30 Minutes

About 5 dozen cookies

¾ cup granulated sugar
¾ cup packed brown sugar
1 cup shortening
3 eggs
1 teaspoon vanilla
2½ cups Pillsbury BEST® all-purpose flour
1 teaspoon baking powder
1 teaspoon baking soda
½ teaspoon salt
1 cup coconut
½ cup old-fashioned oats
½ cup chopped walnuts
12 oz white chocolate baking bars, cut into ¼- to ½-inch chunks

1. Heat oven to 350°F. In large bowl, beat granulated sugar, brown sugar and shortening with electric mixer on medium speed until light and fluffy. Add eggs, one at a time, beating well after each addition. Beat in vanilla. On low speed, beat in flour, baking powder, baking soda and salt until well blended. Stir in remaining ingredients.

2. On ungreased cookie sheets, drop dough by rounded tablespoonfuls 2 inches apart.

3. Bake 10 to 15 minutes or until light golden brown. Cool 1 minute; remove from cookie sheets to cooling racks.

   High Altitude (3500–6500 ft): Decrease baking powder and baking soda to ½ teaspoon each. Bake 8 to 12 minutes.

Chocolate Chunk Cookies: Substitute semisweet chocolate baking bars for the white chocolate bars.

■■■ **take note:** White vanilla baking chips work fine in place of the white chocolate chunks in these cookies.

1 Cookie: Calories 120; Total Fat 7g (Saturated Fat 2.5g; Trans Fat 0.5g); Cholesterol 10mg; Sodium 60mg; Total Carbohydrate 14g (Dietary Fiber 0g) **Exchanges:** 1 Other Carbohydrate, 1½ Fat **Carbohydrate Choices:** 1

cherry winks

Ruth Derousseau | Rice Lake, WI | Bake-Off® Contest 02, 1950

Prep Time: 1 Hour 20 Minutes
Start to Finish: 1 Hour 20 Minutes

About 5 dozen cookies

1 cup sugar
¾ cup shortening
2 tablespoons milk
1 teaspoon vanilla
2 eggs
2¼ cups Pillsbury BEST all-
  purpose flour
1 teaspoon baking powder
½ teaspoon baking soda
½ teaspoon salt
1 cup chopped pecans
1 cup chopped dates
⅓ cup chopped maraschino
  cherries, patted dry with paper
  towels
1½ cups coarsely crushed corn
  flakes cereal
15 maraschino cherries,
  quartered

1 In large bowl, beat sugar and shortening with electric mixer on medium speed, scraping bowl occasionally, until well blended. Beat in milk, vanilla and eggs. On low speed, beat in flour, baking powder, baking soda and salt, scraping bowl occasionally, until dough forms. Stir in pecans, dates and ⅓ cup chopped cherries. If necessary, cover with plastic wrap and refrigerate 15 minutes for easier handling.

2 Heat oven to 375°F. Spray cookie sheets with cooking spray. Drop dough by rounded teaspoonfuls into cereal; coat thoroughly. Shape into balls. Place 2 inches apart on cookie sheets. Lightly press maraschino cherry quarter into top of each ball.

3 Bake 10 to 15 minutes or until light golden brown. Cool 1 minute; remove from cookie sheets to cooling racks.

High Altitude (3500–6500 ft): No change.

1 Cookie: Calories 80; Total Fat 4g (Saturated Fat 1g; Trans Fat 0g); Cholesterol 5mg; Sodium 45mg; Total Carbohydrate 11g (Dietary Fiber 0g) **Exchanges:** ½ Other Carbohydrate, 1 Fat **Carbohydrate Choices:** 1

raspberry-filled brownie delights

Teresa Ralston | New Albany, OH | Bake-Off® Contest 43, 2008

Prep Time: 35 Minutes
Start to Finish: 1 Hour 20 Minutes

1 dozen sandwich cookies

>> 1 box (15.5 oz) Pillsbury® Fudge
   Supreme chocolate chunk
   brownie mix
¼ cup Pillsbury BEST all-purpose
   flour
½ cup butter or margarine,
   melted
1 egg
1 teaspoon vanilla
¼ cup plus 2 tablespoons red
   raspberry preserves
2 to 4 teaspoons powdered sugar
12 fresh raspberries (about ½ cup)

1. Heat oven to 375°F. In large bowl, stir together brownie mix and flour. Add butter, egg and vanilla; stir until blended. Let dough stand 15 minutes for easier handling.

2. Shape dough into 24 (about 1½-inch) balls (dough will be soft). On ungreased large cookie sheet, place balls 2 inches apart.

3. Bake 10 to 13 minutes or until set and tops appear dry. Cool on cookie sheet 1 minute; remove from cookie sheet to cooling racks. Cool completely, about 30 minutes.

4. Spread 1½ teaspoons preserves on bottom of 1 cookie; top with another cookie, bottom side down. Repeat with remaining cookies. Sprinkle powdered sugar through fine-mesh strainer or sieve over cookies. Place on serving platter; garnish as desired with raspberries.

High Altitude (3500–6500 ft): Heat oven to 350°F. Decrease butter to ⅓ cup.

1 Sandwich Cookie: Calories 280; Total Fat 13g (Saturated Fat 7g; Trans Fat 1g); Cholesterol 35mg; Sodium 105mg; Total Carbohydrate 39g (Dietary Fiber 0g) **Exchanges:** ½ Starch, 2 Other Carbohydrate, 2½ Fat **Carbohydrate Choices:** 2½

snappy turtle cookies

Beatrice Harlib | Lincolnwood, IL | Bake-Off® Contest 04, 1952

Prep Time: 1 Hour 25 Minutes
Start to Finish: 2 Hours 25 Minutes

About 3½ dozen cookies

COOKIES
½ cup packed brown sugar
½ cup butter or margarine, softened
¼ teaspoon vanilla
⅛ teaspoon maple flavor, if desired
1 egg
1 egg, separated
1½ cups Pillsbury BEST all-purpose flour
¼ teaspoon baking soda
¼ teaspoon salt
1 cup pecan halves, each broken lengthwise into 2 pieces

FROSTING
⅓ cup semisweet chocolate chips
3 tablespoons milk
1 tablespoon butter or margarine
1 cup powdered sugar

1. In large bowl, beat brown sugar and ½ cup butter with electric mixer on medium speed, scraping bowl occasionally, until light and fluffy. Beat in vanilla, maple flavor, 1 whole egg and 1 egg yolk until well blended. On low speed, beat in flour, baking soda and salt. Cover with plastic wrap; refrigerate at least 1 hour for easier handling.

2. Heat oven to 350°F. Spray cookie sheets with cooking spray. Arrange pecan pieces in groups of 5 on cookie sheets to resemble head and legs of turtle. In small bowl, beat egg white with fork or wire whisk. Shape dough into 1-inch balls. Dip bottoms in beaten egg white; press lightly onto pecans (tips of pecans should show).

3. Bake 10 to 12 minutes or until edges are light golden brown. Immediately remove from cookie sheets to cooling racks. Cool completely, about 15 minutes.

4. Meanwhile, in 1-quart saucepan, heat chocolate chips, milk and 1 tablespoon butter over low heat, stirring constantly, until chips are melted and mixture is smooth. Remove from heat. Stir in powdered sugar. If necessary, add additional powdered sugar until frosting is spreadable. Frost cookies. Let frosting set before storing in tightly covered container.

High Altitude (3500–6500 ft): No change.

1 Cookie: Calories 90; Total Fat 5g (Saturated Fat 2g; Trans Fat 0g); Cholesterol 15mg; Sodium 45mg; Total Carbohydrate 10g (Dietary Fiber 0g) **Exchanges:** ½ Starch, 1 Fat **Carbohydrate Choices:** ½

peanut blossoms

Freda Smith | Gibsonburg, OH | Bake-Off® Contest 09, 1957

Prep Time: 1 Hour
Start to Finish: 1 Hour

About 4 dozen cookies

1¾ cups Pillsbury BEST all-
  purpose flour
½ cup granulated sugar
½ cup packed brown sugar
1 teaspoon baking soda
½ teaspoon salt
½ cup shortening
½ cup peanut butter
2 tablespoons milk
1 teaspoon vanilla
1 egg
¼ cup granulated sugar
48 milk chocolate candy drops or
  pieces, unwrapped

1   Heat oven to 375°F. In large bowl, beat flour, ½ cup granulated sugar, the brown sugar, baking soda, salt, shortening, peanut butter, milk, vanilla and egg with electric mixer on low speed, scraping bowl occasionally, until stiff dough forms.

2   Place ¼ cup granulated sugar in small bowl. Shape dough into 1-inch balls; roll in granulated sugar. On ungreased cookie sheets, place balls 2 inches apart.

3   Bake 10 to 12 minutes or until golden brown. Immediately top each cookie with 1 chocolate candy, pressing down firmly so cookie cracks around edge. Remove from cookie sheets to cooling racks.

High Altitude (3500–6500 ft): No change.

1 Cookie: Calories 100; Total Fat 5g
(Saturated Fat 1.5g; Trans Fat 0g); Cholesterol
5mg; Sodium 70mg; Total Carbohydrate
11g (Dietary Fiber 0g) **Exchanges:** 1 Other
Carbohydrate, 1 Fat **Carbohydrate Choices:** 1

fudgy chocolate–peanut butter thumbprints

Pillsbury
Bake-Off®

Stephanie Hollowell | Dallas, TX | Bake-Off® Contest 43, 2008

Prep Time: 1 Hour
Start to Finish: 1 Hour

2 dozen cookies

COOKIES

>> **1 box (20 oz) Pillsbury Fudge Supreme chocolate frosted brownie mix**
½ **cup extra-crunchy peanut butter**
2 eggs
1 teaspoon vanilla
⅔ **cup milk chocolate chips**

TOPPING
Frosting packet from brownie mix
⅓ **cup extra-crunchy peanut butter**
¼ **cup butter or margarine, softened**
2 tablespoons dry-roasted peanuts, finely chopped

1 Heat oven to 350°F. Lightly spray large cookie sheets with cooking spray, or line with cooking parchment paper.

2 Reserve frosting packet from brownie mix. In large bowl, beat brownie mix, ½ cup peanut butter, the eggs and vanilla with electric mixer on low speed 20 seconds. Beat on high speed 30 to 40 seconds or until completely mixed. Stir in chocolate chips.

3 Drop 24 heaping tablespoons of dough 2 inches apart onto cookie sheets. Press thumb into center of each cookie to make indentation, but do not press all the way to the cookie sheet (if dough sticks to thumb, spray thumb with cooking spray). Bake 9 to 11 minutes or until almost no indentation remains when touched. Cool 1 minute; remove from cookie sheets to cooling racks. Cool completely, about 20 minutes.

4 In small bowl, beat contents of reserved frosting packet, ⅓ cup peanut butter and the butter with electric mixer on medium speed until smooth. Fill each thumbprint indentation with 2 teaspoons frosting mixture, spreading slightly; sprinkle with peanuts. Let stand until frosting mixture is set. Store loosely covered in single layer.

High Altitude (3500–6500 ft): No change.

1 Cookie: Calories 120; Total Fat 9g (Saturated Fat 3g; Trans Fat 0g); Cholesterol 20mg; Sodium 60mg; Total Carbohydrate 6g (Dietary Fiber 0g) **Exchanges:** ½ Other Carbohydrate, ½ High-Fat Meat, 1 Fat
Carbohydrate Choices: ½

double-delight peanut butter cookies

Carolyn Gurtz | Gaithersburg, MD | Bake-Off® Contest 43, 2008

Prep Time: 45 Minutes
Start to Finish: 45 Minutes

2 dozen cookies

¼ **cup dry-roasted peanuts, finely chopped**
¼ **cup granulated sugar**
½ **teaspoon ground cinnamon**
½ **cup creamy peanut butter**
½ **cup powdered sugar**
>> 1 **roll (16.5 oz) Pillsbury refrigerated peanut butter cookies, well chilled**

1 Heat oven to 375°F. In small bowl, mix chopped peanuts, granulated sugar and cinnamon; set aside.

2 In another small bowl, stir peanut butter and powdered sugar until completely blended. Shape mixture into 24 (1-inch) balls.

3 Cut roll of cookie dough into 12 slices. Cut each slice in half crosswise to make 24 pieces; flatten slightly. Shape 1 cookie dough piece around 1 peanut butter ball, covering completely. Repeat with remaining dough and balls.

4 Roll each covered ball in peanut mixture; gently pat mixture completely onto balls. On ungreased large cookie sheets, place balls 2 inches apart. Spray bottom of drinking glass with cooking spray; press into remaining peanut mixture. Flatten each ball to ½-inch thickness with bottom of glass. Sprinkle any remaining peanut mixture evenly on tops of cookies; gently press into dough.

5 Bake 7 to 12 minutes or until edges are golden brown. Cool 1 minute; remove from cookie sheets to cooling racks. Store tightly covered.

High Altitude (3500–6500 ft): No change.

1 Cookie: Calories 150; Total Fat 7g (Saturated Fat 1.5g; Trans Fat 0.5g); Cholesterol 0mg; Sodium 125mg; Total Carbohydrate 17g (Dietary Fiber 0g) **Exchanges:** 1 Starch, 1½ Fat **Carbohydrate Choices:** 1

fudgy peanut butter sandwich cookies

Beverley Rossell | **Morgantown, IN** | **Bake-Off® Contest 43, 2008**

Prep Time: 1 Hour 10 Minutes
Start to Finish: 1 Hour 55 Minutes

1½ dozen sandwich cookies

COOKIES
1 roll (16.5 oz) Pillsbury refrigerated peanut butter cookies
1 cup plus 2 tablespoons honey-roasted peanuts, coarsely ground

PEANUT BUTTER FUDGE FILLING
½ cup butter or margarine
½ cup creamy peanut butter
2 teaspoons vanilla
2⅓ cups powdered sugar

GANACHE
1 cup semisweet chocolate chips
2 tablespoons whipping cream

1. In large bowl, break up cookie dough. Mix in 1 cup of the peanuts. Cover; refrigerate about 30 minutes or until well chilled.

2. Heat oven to 375°F. Spray cookie sheets with cooking spray, or line with cooking parchment paper. Shape dough into 36 (1¼-inch) balls. Place balls 2 inches apart on cookie sheets. Flatten to ½-inch thickness with lightly floured metal spatula or drinking glass. Bake 9 to 11 minutes or until edges are golden brown. Cool 5 minutes; remove from cookie sheets to cooling racks. Cool completely, about 30 minutes.

3. Meanwhile, in 2-quart saucepan, melt butter and peanut butter over medium heat, stirring occasionally. Remove from heat; stir in vanilla. Cool 1 minute. Stir in powdered sugar. When cool enough to handle, knead filling several times until powdered sugar is thoroughly blended. Shape into log, about 9 inches long and 2 inches in diameter. Cut into 18 (½-inch) slices, reshaping slices into round shape if necessary. Cover with plastic wrap; set aside.

4. When ready to assemble cookies, place 1 filling slice on bottom of 1 cookie; top with another cookie, bottom side down, and press together slightly. Repeat with remaining cookies.

5. In medium microwavable bowl, microwave chocolate chips and whipping cream uncovered on High about 1 minute, stirring twice, until melted. Spoon heaping 1 teaspoonful on top of each cookie. Sprinkle with remaining ground peanuts. Let stand 10 minutes or until ganache is set. Store tightly covered in single layer at room temperature.

High Altitude (3500–6500 ft): No change.

take note: To grind peanuts, place in food processor bowl with metal blade. Cover and process with on-and-off pulses until coarsely ground.

1 Sandwich Cookie: Calories 380; Total Fat 22g (Saturated Fat 8g; Trans Fat 1g); Cholesterol 20mg; Sodium 190mg; Total Carbohydrate 40g (Dietary Fiber 2g) **Exchanges:** ½ Starch, 2 Other Carbohydrate, ½ High-Fat Meat, 3½ Fat **Carbohydrate Choices:** 2½

choco–peanut butter cups

Ronna Farley | Rockville, MD | Bake-Off® Contest 42, 2006

Prep Time: 40 Minutes
Start to Finish: 1 Hour 40 Minutes

24 cookie cups

>> **1 roll (16.5 oz) Pillsbury refrigerated peanut butter cookies**
1 cup white vanilla baking chips (6 oz)
1½ cups creamy peanut butter
1 cup semisweet chocolate chips (6 oz)
4 oats 'n honey crunchy granola bars (2 pouches from 8.9-oz box), crushed (¾ cup)

1 Heat oven to 350°F. Spray 24 mini muffin cups with cooking spray.

2 Cut cookie dough into 24 slices. Press 1 slice in bottom and up side of each mini muffin cup, forming ¼-inch rim above top of cup (dust fingers with flour if necessary). Bake 10 to 15 minutes or until edges are deep golden brown. Cool in pans on cooling racks 5 minutes. With tip of handle of wooden spoon, press dough down in center of each cup to make room for 2 tablespoons filling.

3 Meanwhile, in 2-quart saucepan, melt baking chips and ¾ cup of the peanut butter over low heat, stirring constantly. Spoon about 1 tablespoon mixture into each dough-lined cup. Refrigerate 10 minutes.

4 In another 2-quart saucepan, melt chocolate chips and remaining ¾ cup peanut butter over low heat, stirring constantly. Spoon about 1 tablespoon chocolate mixture on top of peanut butter mixture in each cup. Sprinkle crushed granola bars over top of each. Refrigerate about 1 hour or until set. Remove from muffin cups before serving.

High Altitude (3500–6500 ft): Break up cookie dough into bowl; knead or stir ¼ cup all-purpose flour into dough. Divide dough into 24 pieces; press 1 piece in each cup.

take note: To easily crush granola bars, do not unwrap them. Crush them in the pouches with a rolling pin or the smooth side of a meat mallet.

1 Cookie Cup: Calories 290; Total Fat 17g (Saturated Fat 6g; Trans Fat 0.5g); Cholesterol 0mg; Sodium 200mg; Total Carbohydrate 26g (Dietary Fiber 1g) **Exchanges:** 1 Starch, ½ Other Carbohydrate, ½ High-Fat Meat, 2½ Fat **Carbohydrate Choices:** 2

butterscotch crackles

Prep Time: 1 Hour 30 Minutes
Start to Finish: 1 Hour 30 Minutes

4 dozen cookies

>> **2 rolls (16.5 oz each) Pillsbury
refrigerated sugar cookies**
**2 cups Wheaties® cereal, crushed
(1 cup)**
1 cup butterscotch chips (6 oz)
1 cup flaked coconut
½ cup powdered sugar

1 Let cookie dough stand at room temperature to soften slightly, about 20 minutes.

2 Heat oven to 350°F. Spray cookie sheets with cooking spray. In large bowl, break up cookie dough. Stir or knead in crushed cereal, butterscotch chips and coconut until well blended.

3 Place powdered sugar in small bowl. Shape dough into 48 (1-inch) balls; roll in powdered sugar and place 2 inches apart on cookie sheets.

4 Bake 11 to 15 minutes or until edges are golden brown. Cool 1 minute; remove from cookie sheets to cooling racks.

High Altitude (3500–6500 ft): No change.

1 Cookie: Calories 130; Total Fat 6g
(Saturated Fat 2.5g; Trans Fat 1g); Cholesterol
5mg; Sodium 80mg; Total Carbohydrate 18g
(Dietary Fiber 0g) **Exchanges:** 1 Starch, 1 Fat
Carbohydrate Choices: 1

candy bar cookies

Alice Reese | Minneapolis, MN | Bake-Off® Contest 13, 1961

Prep Time: 1 Hour 15 Minutes
Start to Finish: 1 Hour 15 Minutes

About 40 cookies

CRUST
¾ cup powdered sugar
¾ cup butter or margarine, softened
2 tablespoons whipping cream
1 teaspoon vanilla
2 cups Pillsbury BEST all-purpose flour

FILLING
21 caramels, unwrapped
3 tablespoons whipping cream
3 tablespoons butter or margarine
¾ cup powdered sugar
¾ cup chopped pecans

GLAZE
⅓ cup semisweet chocolate chips
1 tablespoon whipping cream
2 teaspoons butter or margarine
3 tablespoons powdered sugar
1 teaspoon vanilla
40 pecan halves (½ cup), if desired

1. In large bowl, mix all crust ingredients except flour with spoon until well blended. Stir in flour until dough forms. If necessary, cover dough with plastic wrap and refrigerate 1 hour for easier handling.

2. Heat oven to 325°F. On well-floured surface, roll half of dough at a time into 10×8-inch rectangle, using lightly floured rolling pin. With pastry wheel or knife, cut into 2-inch squares. Place ½ inch apart on ungreased cookie sheets.

3. Bake 10 to 13 minutes or until set. Immediately remove from cookie sheets to cooling racks. Cool completely, about 15 minutes.

4. In 2-quart saucepan, heat caramels, 3 tablespoons whipping cream and 3 tablespoons butter over low heat, stirring frequently, until caramels are melted and mixture is smooth. Remove from heat. Stir in ¾ cup powdered sugar and the chopped pecans (add additional whipping cream, a few drops at a time, if needed for desired spreading consistency). Spread 1 teaspoon warm filling on each cookie square.

5. In 1-quart saucepan, heat chocolate chips, 1 tablespoon whipping cream and 2 teaspoons butter over low heat, stirring frequently, until chips are melted and mixture is smooth. REMOVE FROM HEAT. Stir in 3 tablespoons powdered sugar and 1 teaspoon vanilla. Spread glaze evenly over caramel filling on each cookie. Top each with pecan half.

High Altitude (3500–6500 ft): No change.

1 Cookie: Calories 130; Total Fat 8g (Saturated Fat 4g; Trans Fat 0g); Cholesterol 15mg; Sodium 45mg; Total Carbohydrate 15g (Dietary Fiber 0g) **Exchanges:** 1 Other Carbohydrate, 1½ Fat **Carbohydrate Choices:** 1

jumbo honey-roasted peanut butter sandwich cookies

Pillsbury Bake-Off

Karry Edwards | Sandy, UT | Bake-Off® Contest 43, 2008

Prep Time: 25 Minutes
Start to Finish: 1 Hour 10 Minutes

About 8 sandwich cookies

2 packages (8 oz each) cream cheese, softened
½ cup creamy peanut butter
2 tablespoons honey
1 cup powdered sugar
1 roll (16.5 oz) Pillsbury refrigerated peanut butter cookies
¾ to 1 cup honey-roasted dry-roasted peanuts, coarsely chopped

1 In large bowl, beat cream cheese, peanut butter and honey with electric mixer on medium speed until smooth. Add powdered sugar; beat just until smooth. Cover; refrigerate at least 1 hour while baking and cooling cookies.

2 Heat oven to 350°F. Make cookies as directed on package. Cool completely.

3 Spread ⅓ cup cream cheese mixture on bottom of 1 cookie; top with another cookie, bottom side down. Press cookies together slightly so cream cheese mixture just extends past edges of cookies. Roll edge of cream cheese mixture in chopped peanuts to generously coat. Repeat with remaining cookies.

4 Serve immediately, or store in single layer tightly covered in refrigerator up to 4 hours (cookies stored longer become very soft).

High Altitude (3500–6500 ft): No change.

1 Sandwich Cookie: Calories 730; Total Fat 47g (Saturated Fat 18g; Trans Fat 2.5g); Cholesterol 70mg; Sodium 560mg; Total Carbohydrate 60g (Dietary Fiber 2g) **Exchanges:** 1 Starch, 3 Other Carbohydrate, 2 High-Fat Meat, 6 Fat **Carbohydrate Choices:** 4

split seconds

Robert E. Fellows | **Silver Spring, MD** | **Bake-Off® Contest 06, 1954**

Prep Time: 1 Hour 15 Minutes
Start to Finish: 1 Hour 15 Minutes

About 4 dozen cookies

⅔ **cup sugar**
¾ **cup butter or margarine,
   softened**
2 **teaspoons vanilla**
1 **egg**
2 **cups Pillsbury BEST all-purpose
   flour**
½ **teaspoon baking powder**
½ **cup red jelly or preserves**

1 Heat oven to 350°F. In large bowl, beat sugar and butter with electric mixer on medium speed until light and fluffy. Beat in vanilla and egg until well blended. On low speed, beat in flour and baking powder until dough forms.

2 Divide dough into 4 equal parts. On lightly floured surface, shape each part into 12×¾-inch roll; place on ungreased cookie sheets. With handle of wooden spoon or finger, make indentation about ½ inch wide and ¼ inch deep lengthwise down center of each roll. Fill each with 2 tablespoons jelly.

3 Bake 15 to 20 minutes or until light golden brown. Cool slightly, 3 to 5 minutes. Cut each baked roll diagonally into 12 cookies; remove from cookie sheets to cooling racks.

High Altitude (3500–6500 ft): No change.

take note: This cookie recipe may have gotten its clever name because it takes only a "split second" to form the indentation that is filled with yummy red jelly.

1 Cookie: Calories 70; Total Fat 3g (Saturated Fat 2g; Trans Fat 0g); Cholesterol 10mg; Sodium 30mg; Total Carbohydrate 9g (Dietary Fiber 0g) **Exchanges:** ½ Starch, ½ Fat
Carbohydrate Choices: ½

peanuttiest peanut butter brownie bars

Sheilah Fiola | Kent, WA | Bake-Off® Contest 43, 2008

Prep Time: 30 Minutes
Start to Finish: 3 Hours 55 Minutes

24 bars

- **1 box (13.3 oz) Pillsbury Fudge Supreme peanut butter swirl brownie mix**
- **2 cups crushed chocolate or regular graham crackers (28 squares)**
- **½ cup plus 3 tablespoons butter or margarine**
- **1 can (14 oz) sweetened condensed milk (not evaporated)**
- **⅓ cup creamy peanut butter**
- **1¼ cups peanut butter chips**
- **¾ cup milk chocolate chips**
- **1 cup Spanish peanuts, finely chopped**

1 Heat oven to 350°F (325°F for dark or nonstick pan). Lightly spray bottom and sides of 13×9-inch pan with cooking spray.

2 In large bowl, stir dry brownie mix and graham cracker crumbs until well mixed; set aside.

3 Into medium microwavable bowl, squeeze peanut butter from peanut butter packet (from brownie mix). Add butter. Microwave uncovered on High 1 minute to 1 minute 30 seconds, stirring once, until butter is melted. Stir until smooth.

4 Pour peanut butter mixture over brownie mixture; stir until well mixed. Press evenly in pan.

5 In same medium microwavable bowl, mix condensed milk, ⅓ cup peanut butter and ½ cup of the peanut butter chips. Microwave uncovered on High 1 minute, stirring once, until mixture is melted. Stir until smooth.

6 Gently pour milk mixture evenly over brownie layer in pan; spread evenly. Sprinkle remaining ¾ cup peanut butter chips, the chocolate chips and peanuts over milk mixture; press in lightly.

7 Bake 18 to 22 minutes or until edges are golden brown and center is just set when lightly touched (do not overbake). Cool completely in pan on cooling rack, about 3 hours. For bars, cut into 6 rows by 4 rows.

High Altitude (3500–6500 ft): Bake 25 to 30 minutes.

1 Bar: Calories 350; Total Fat 20g (Saturated Fat 9g; Trans Fat 0.5g); Cholesterol 20mg; Sodium 190mg; Total Carbohydrate 35g (Dietary Fiber 1g) **Exchanges:** 1 Starch, 1½ Other Carbohydrate, ½ High-Fat Meat, 3 Fat **Carbohydrate Choices:** 2

mexican chocolate crunch brownies

Valerie Schucht | Glastonbury, CT | Bake-Off® Contest 43, 2008

Prep Time: 20 Minutes
Start to Finish: 3 Hours

24 brownies

1 box (12.8 oz) Cinnamon Toast Crunch® cereal (about 8 cups)
½ cup butter or margarine, melted
1 tablespoon corn syrup
>> 1 box (19.5 oz) Pillsbury Brownie Classics traditional fudge brownie mix
½ cup vegetable oil
¼ cup water
2 eggs
½ teaspoon ground cinnamon
1⅓ cups semisweet chocolate chips
3 tablespoons cinnamon-sugar (from 3.62-oz jar)

1 Heat oven to 350°F. Spray bottom and sides of 13×9-inch pan with cooking spray. Place cereal in food processor bowl with metal blade (crush cereal in 2 batches if necessary). Cover; process until finely crushed (about 4 cups). Or place cereal in large resealable food-storage plastic bag; crush with rolling pin.

2 In large bowl, stir butter and corn syrup until well blended. Add crushed cereal; mix thoroughly. Press evenly in pan.

3 In large bowl, make brownie mix as directed on box, using oil, water and eggs and adding cinnamon. Stir in ⅔ cup of the chocolate chips. Pour brownie batter over cereal mixture. Sprinkle remaining ⅔ cup chocolate chips evenly over batter.

4 Bake 20 minutes. Sprinkle cinnamon-sugar evenly over brownies. Bake 14 to 18 minutes longer or until brownies are set when lightly touched in center. Cool 10 minutes; loosen edges but do not cut. Cool completely, about 2 hours. For brownies, cut into 6 rows by 4 rows.

High Altitude (3500–6500 ft): In step 2, bake crust 5 to 8 minutes. Make brownie mix following High Altitude directions on box.

take note: To substitute for the purchased cinnamon-sugar, mix 3 tablespoons sugar with ½ teaspoon ground cinnamon.

1 Brownie: Calories 280; Total Fat 15g (Saturated Fat 5g; Trans Fat 0g); Cholesterol 25mg; Sodium 190mg; Total Carbohydrate 35g (Dietary Fiber 1g) **Exchanges:** ½ Starch, 1½ Other Carbohydrate, 3 Fat **Carbohydrate Choices:** 2

tropical fruit bars

Prep Time: 15 Minutes
Start to Finish: 2 Hours 25 Minutes

36 bars

>>
- **1 package (16 oz) Pillsbury Big Deluxe Classics® refrigerated white chocolate chunk macadamia nut cookies**
- **1 can (14 oz) sweetened condensed milk (not evaporated)**
- **1 container (6 oz) 99% fat-free piña colada yogurt**
- **1 bag (6 to 7 oz) mixed tropical dried fruits**
- **1 jar (6 oz) dry-roasted macadamia nuts, coarsely chopped**
- **¾ cup white vanilla baking chips**
- **1 cup flaked coconut**

1 Heat oven to 350°F (325°F for dark pan). Spray bottom and sides of 13×9-inch pan with cooking spray. Place cookie dough rounds in pan. With floured fingers, press dough in pan to form crust.

2 In medium bowl, mix condensed milk and yogurt until well blended. Spread over crust to edges of pan. Sprinkle with remaining ingredients in order listed.

3 Bake 30 to 40 minutes or until edges are golden brown. Cool completely, about 1 hour 30 minutes. For bars, cut into 6 rows by 6 rows. Store covered in refrigerator.

High Altitude (3500–6500 ft): Bake 35 to 45 minutes.

1 Bar: Calories 190; Total Fat 10g (Saturated Fat 4g; Trans Fat 0.5g); Cholesterol 5mg; Sodium 80mg; Total Carbohydrate 22g (Dietary Fiber 1g) **Exchanges:** ½ Starch, 1 Other Carbohydrate, 2 Fat **Carbohydrate Choices:** 1½

Simple Sandwich Cookies

Bake a 16-ounce package of ready-to-bake refrigerated cookies. Spread half the baked cookies with a filling; top with remaining cookies and gently press together.

Linzer Cookies: Spread seedless raspberry jam between pairs of cookies; sprinkle tops with powdered sugar. Melt 1 cup semisweet chocolate chips and 1 teaspoon shortening until smooth; drizzle over powdered sugar.

Cool "Wiches": Spoon slightly softened ice cream, frozen yogurt or sherbet between pairs of cookies. Roll edges in chopped nuts, mini chocolate chips or decors if desired. Wrap in plastic wrap or foil; freeze.

PB&J Cookies: Mix ⅓ cup vanilla creamy ready-to-spread frosting and 2 tablespoons peanut butter until smooth. Spread on bottoms of half the cookies; top with favorite jelly and remaining cookies.

S'more Cookies: Mix ½ cup powdered sugar and 1½ cups marshmallow creme. Place on surface sprinkled with powdered sugar. Knead in additional 1½ cups powdered sugar. Shape into two 8-inch ropes; cut each into 2-inch pieces. Place 1 piece between pair of cookies.

orangeburst cookie bars

Betty Eder | **Las Vegas, NV** | **Bake-Off® Contest 38, 1998**

Prep Time: 15 Minutes
Start to Finish: 1 Hour 40 Minutes

24 bars

>> 1 roll (16.5 oz) Pillsbury
   refrigerated sugar cookies
1 cup chopped hazelnuts
   (filberts) or almonds
½ cup granulated sugar
5 teaspoons Pillsbury BEST
   all-purpose flour
⅓ cup light corn syrup
1 tablespoon grated orange peel
¼ cup orange juice
1 tablespoon butter or margarine,
   melted
1 egg
1 to 3 tablespoons powdered
   sugar, if desired

1 Heat oven to 375°F. Cut dough into ½-inch slices. In bottom of ungreased 13×9-inch pan, arrange slices. With floured fingers, press dough evenly in bottom of pan to form crust. Sprinkle with ½ cup of the hazelnuts; press firmly into dough. Bake 10 to 12 minutes or until dough is puffed.

2 Meanwhile, in medium bowl, mix granulated sugar and flour. Stir in corn syrup, orange peel, orange juice, butter and egg with wire whisk until smooth. Stir in remaining ½ cup hazelnuts.

3 Remove partially baked crust from oven. Carefully pour corn syrup mixture over crust. Reduce oven temperature to 350°F.

4 Bake 18 to 23 minutes longer or until edges are golden brown and filling is set. Cool 10 minutes. Sprinkle with powdered sugar. Cool completely, about 50 minutes. For bars, cut into 6 rows by 4 rows.

High Altitude (3500–6500 ft): In large bowl, knead or stir 3 tablespoons all-purpose flour into cookie dough; press in pan. Bake crust 14 to 16 minutes. Bake filling 20 to 25 minutes.

1 Bar: Calories 160; Total Fat 8g (Saturated Fat 1.5g; Trans Fat 1g); Cholesterol 15mg; Sodium 70mg; Total Carbohydrate 21g (Dietary Fiber 0g) **Exchanges:** ½ Starch, 1 Other Carbohydrate, 1½ Fat **Carbohydrate Choices:** 1½

mocha-walnut bars with dark chocolate ganache

Pillsbury Bake-Off

Elizabeth Bennett | **Mill Creek, WA** | **Bake-Off® Contest 43, 2008**

Prep Time: 30 Minutes
Start to Finish: 3 Hours 10 Minutes

24 bars

2½ cups very finely chopped walnuts

6 tablespoons sugar

6 tablespoons butter or margarine, melted

1 roll (16.5 oz) Pillsbury refrigerated sugar cookies

1 tablespoon instant espresso coffee granules

1½ cups dark chocolate chips

¼ cup plus 2 tablespoons whipping cream

1 Heat oven to 350°F. In medium bowl, stir walnuts, sugar and butter until moistened. Press mixture evenly on bottom of ungreased 13×9-inch pan or 12×8-inch (2-quart) glass baking dish. Bake 8 to 15 minutes or until edges are just golden brown. Cool 30 minutes.

2 In large bowl, knead cookie dough and espresso granules until blended. Drop small spoonfuls of dough evenly over walnut crust. Gently press dough together evenly over crust. (If dough is sticky, use floured fingers.)

3 Bake 20 to 25 minutes or until golden brown. Cool 30 minutes.

4 In medium microwavable bowl, microwave chocolate chips and whipping cream uncovered on High 1 minute, stirring after 30 seconds; stir until chips are melted and mixture is smooth. Spread chocolate mixture over bars. Refrigerate 1 hour. For bars, cut into 6 rows by 4 rows. Cover and refrigerate any remaining bars.

High Altitude (3500–6500 ft): No change.

1 Bar: Calories 290; Total Fat 20g (Saturated Fat 6g; Trans Fat 1g); Cholesterol 20mg; Sodium 85mg; Total Carbohydrate 24g (Dietary Fiber 1g) **Exchanges:** 1½ Other Carbohydrate, ½ High-Fat Meat, 3 Fat **Carbohydrate Choices:** 1½

apricot-caramel-coconut bars

Linda Hickam | Healdsburg, CA | Bake-Off® Contest 43, 2008

Prep Time: 10 Minutes
Start to Finish: 3 Hours

36 bars

1 cup slivered blanched almonds
2 cups Pillsbury BEST all-purpose unbleached flour
½ cup sugar
1 cup butter or margarine, cut up
1 cup apricot preserves
⅓ cup caramel topping
¾ cup unsweetened or sweetened shredded coconut

1 Heat oven to 350°F.

2 In food processor bowl with metal blade, place almonds. Cover; process with on-and-off pulses until finely chopped. Add flour, sugar and butter to almonds. Cover; process with on-and-off pulses until mixture looks like coarse crumbs. (Or, finely chop almonds. In large bowl, mix chopped almonds, flour and sugar; cut in butter with pastry blender until mixture looks like coarse crumbs.)

3 In bottom of ungreased 13×9-inch pan, evenly press half of crumb mixture (about 2½ cups).

4 In medium bowl, mix preserves, caramel topping and coconut. Spread over crumb mixture to within ½ inch of edges. Sprinkle remaining crumb mixture evenly over apricot mixture to edges of pan.

5 Bake 40 to 50 minutes or until edges are golden brown. Cool completely, about 2 hours. For bars, cut into 6 rows by 6 rows.

High Altitude (3500–6500 ft): No change.

1 Bar: Calories 140; Total Fat 8g (Saturated Fat 4.5g; Trans Fat 0g); Cholesterol 15mg; Sodium 50mg; Total Carbohydrate 16g (Dietary Fiber 0g) **Exchanges:** ½ Starch, ½ Other Carbohydrate, 1½ Fat **Carbohydrate Choices:** 1

nutty chocolate pretzel bars

Patrice Hurd | Bemidji, MN | Bake-Off® Contest 40, 2002

Prep Time: 20 Minutes
Start to Finish: 1 Hour 45 Minutes

36 bars

1 can (10 oz) deluxe salted mixed nuts (coarsely chop Brazil nuts)

>> **1 roll (16.5 oz) Pillsbury refrigerated sugar cookies**

1 cup toffee bits

1½ cups milk chocolate chips

⅓ cup butterscotch chips

⅓ cup creamy peanut butter

1 cup coarsely chopped salted pretzels

1 oz vanilla-flavored candy coating (almond bark), chopped, or 2 tablespoons white vanilla baking chips

1 Heat oven to 375°F. Spray bottom and sides of 13×9-inch pan with cooking spray. Spread nuts in bottom of pan. Cut cookie dough into ½-inch slices; place over nuts in pan. With floured fingers, press to form crust. Sprinkle toffee bits over crust; press in lightly.

2 Bake 20 to 25 minutes or until golden brown. Cool 30 minutes.

3 In large microwavable bowl, microwave chocolate chips and butterscotch chips uncovered on High 1 minute 30 seconds to 2 minutes, stirring every 30 seconds, until melted and smooth. Stir in peanut butter until well blended. Fold in pretzels. Spread mixture evenly over baked crust.

4 In small microwavable bowl, microwave candy coating uncovered on High 30 to 60 seconds, stirring every 15 seconds, until melted and smooth. Drizzle over bars. Refrigerate 30 minutes or until coating is set. For bars, cut into 6 rows by 6 rows.

High Altitude (3500–6500 ft): No change.

1 Bar: Calories 210; Total Fat 13g (Saturated Fat 4.5g; Trans Fat 0.5g); Cholesterol 10mg; Sodium 125mg; Total Carbohydrate 20g (Dietary Fiber 1g) **Exchanges:** ½ Starch, 1 Other Carbohydrate, 2½ Fat **Carbohydrate Choices:** 1

salted peanut chews

Gertrude M. Schweitzerhof | Cupertino, CA | Bake-Off® Contest 29, 1980

Prep Time: 35 Minutes
Start to Finish: 1 Hour 35 Minutes

36 bars

CRUST
1½ cups Pillsbury BEST all-purpose flour
⅔ cup packed brown sugar
½ teaspoon baking powder
½ teaspoon salt
¼ teaspoon baking soda
½ cup butter or margarine, softened
1 teaspoon vanilla
2 egg yolks
3 cups miniature marshmallows

TOPPING
⅔ cup corn syrup
¼ cup butter or margarine
2 teaspoons vanilla
1 bag (10 oz) peanut butter chips (1⅔ cups)
2 cups crisp rice cereal
2 cups salted peanuts

1   Heat oven to 350°F. In large bowl, beat all crust ingredients except marshmallows with electric mixer on low speed until crumbly. Press mixture firmly in bottom of ungreased 13×9-inch pan.

2   Bake 12 to 15 minutes or until light golden brown. Immediately sprinkle marshmallows evenly over crust; bake 1 to 2 minutes longer or until marshmallows just begin to puff. Cool while making topping.

3   In 3-quart saucepan, mix all topping ingredients except cereal and peanuts. Heat over low heat, stirring constantly, just until chips are melted and mixture is smooth. Remove from heat. Stir in cereal and peanuts. Immediately spoon warm topping over marshmallows; spread to cover. Refrigerate about 45 minutes or until firm. For bars, cut into 6 rows by 6 rows.

High Altitude (3500–6500 ft): Heat oven to 375°F.

1 Bar: Calories 200; Total Fat 11g (Saturated Fat 3.5g; Trans Fat 0g); Cholesterol 20mg; Sodium 130mg; Total Carbohydrate 22g (Dietary Fiber 1g) **Exchanges:** 1½ Other Carbohydrate, ½ High-Fat Meat, 1½ Fat **Carbohydrate Choices:** 1½

Kathleen Kildsig | Kiel, WI | Bake-Off® Contest 40, 2002

Prep Time: 20 Minutes
Start to Finish: 1 Hour 20 Minutes

36 bars

>> 1 roll (16.5 oz) Pillsbury
   refrigerated chocolate chip
   cookies
1 bag (11.5 oz) milk chocolate
   chips (2 cups)
1 container (16 oz) caramel apple
   dip (1½ cups)
3 cups crisp rice cereal
1¼ cups chopped cashews

1 Heat oven to 350°F. In ungreased 13×9-inch pan, break up cookie dough. With floured fingers, press dough evenly in bottom of pan to form crust.

2 Bake 15 to 18 minutes or until light golden brown. Cool 15 minutes.

3 Meanwhile, in 3- to 4-quart saucepan, heat 1 cup of the chocolate chips and 1 cup of the dip over medium heat, stirring constantly, until melted and smooth. Remove from heat. Stir in cereal and cashews.

4 Spread cereal mixture over crust. In 1-quart saucepan, heat remaining chocolate chips and dip over medium heat, stirring constantly, until melted and smooth. Spread over cereal mixture. Refrigerate about 30 minutes or until chocolate mixture is set. For bars, cut into 6 by 6 rows.

High Altitude (3500–6500 ft): Bake crust 16 to 19 minutes.

1 Bar: Calories 180; Total Fat 8g (Saturated Fat 2.5g; Trans Fat 0.5g); Cholesterol 0mg; Sodium 95mg; Total Carbohydrate 25g (Dietary Fiber 1g) **Exchanges:** ½ Starch, 1 Other Carbohydrate, 1½ Fat **Carbohydrate Choices:** 1½

chewy chocolate–peanut butter bars

Marjorie Bergemann | Greenbelt, MD | Bake-Off® Contest 39, 2000

Prep Time: 15 Minutes
Start to Finish: 2 Hours 45 Minutes

36 bars

>>
1 roll (16.5 oz) Pillsbury refrigerated sugar cookies
1 can (14 oz) sweetened condensed milk (not evaporated)
1 cup crunchy peanut butter
1 teaspoon vanilla
3 egg yolks
1 bag (12 oz) semisweet chocolate chips (2 cups)

1 Heat oven to 350°F. Spray bottom and sides of 13×9-inch pan with cooking spray. Cut cookie dough in half crosswise. Cut each section in half lengthwise. Press dough evenly in bottom of pan to form crust. Bake 10 minutes.

2 Meanwhile, in medium bowl, mix condensed milk, peanut butter, vanilla and egg yolks until smooth.

3 Remove partially baked crust from oven. Spoon milk mixture evenly over crust; carefully spread.

4 Bake 20 to 25 minutes longer or until set. Sprinkle with chocolate chips; let stand 3 minutes to soften. Spread chocolate evenly over top. Cool completely, about 1 hour 30 minutes. Refrigerate about 30 minutes or until chocolate is set. For bars, cut into 6 rows by 6 rows.

High Altitude (3500–6500 ft): Bake crust 12 to 15 minutes.

1 Bar: Calories 190; Total Fat 10g (Saturated Fat 4g; Trans Fat 0.5g); Cholesterol 25mg; Sodium 85mg; Total Carbohydrate 21g (Dietary Fiber 0g) **Exchanges:** ½ Starch, 1 Other Carbohydrate, 2 Fat **Carbohydrate Choices:** 1½

rocky road fudge bars

Mary Wilson | Leesburg, GA | Bake-Off® Contest 23, 1972

Prep Time: 25 Minutes
Start to Finish: 2 Hours

48 bars

CRUST
½ cup butter or margarine
1 oz unsweetened baking
    chocolate, cut into pieces
1 cup Pillsbury BEST all-purpose
    flour
1 cup granulated sugar
1 teaspoon baking powder
1 teaspoon vanilla
2 eggs
¾ cup chopped nuts

FILLING
6 oz cream cheese (from 8-oz
    package), softened
¼ cup butter or margarine,
    softened
½ cup granulated sugar
2 tablespoons Pillsbury BEST
    all-purpose flour
½ teaspoon vanilla
1 egg
¼ cup chopped nuts
1 cup semisweet chocolate chips
2 cups miniature marshmallows

FROSTING
Remaining 2 oz cream cheese
¼ cup butter or margarine
¼ cup milk
1 oz unsweetened baking
    chocolate, cut into pieces
3 cups powdered sugar
1 teaspoon vanilla

1 Bar: Calories 170; Total Fat 9g (Saturated
Fat 5g; Trans Fat 0g); Cholesterol 30mg;
Sodium 60mg; Total Carbohydrate 21g
(Dietary Fiber 0g) **Exchanges:** ½ Starch,
1 Other Carbohydrate, 1½ Fat **Carbohydrate
Choices:** 1½

1 Heat oven to 350°F. Spray bottom and sides of 13×9-inch pan with baking spray with flour. In 2-quart saucepan, melt ½ cup butter and 1 oz baking chocolate over low heat, stirring frequently, until smooth. Remove from heat. Stir in remaining crust ingredients until well mixed. Spread in pan.

2 In small bowl, beat 6 oz cream cheese, ¼ cup butter, ½ cup granulated sugar, 2 tablespoons flour, ½ teaspoon vanilla and 1 egg with electric mixer on medium speed 1 minute, scraping bowl occasionally, until smooth and fluffy. Stir in ¼ cup nuts. Spread over crust in pan; sprinkle evenly with chocolate chips.

3 Bake 25 to 35 minutes or until toothpick inserted in center comes out clean. Immediately sprinkle with marshmallows.

4 Bake 2 minutes longer. Meanwhile, in 3-quart saucepan, cook remaining 2 oz cream cheese, ¼ cup butter, the milk and 1 oz baking chocolate over low heat, stirring frequently, until well blended. Remove from heat. Stir in powdered sugar and 1 teaspoon vanilla until smooth. Immediately pour frosting over puffed marshmallows. Refrigerate about 1 hour or until firm. For bars, cut into 8 rows by 6 rows. Cover and refrigerate any remaining bars.

High Altitude (3500–6500 ft): No change.

take note: To quickly soften cream cheese, remove from wrapper and place on microwavable plate. Microwave uncovered on High about 15 seconds or just until softened.

coconut-pecan-fudge bars

Jenna Reynolds | Silverdale, WA | Bake-Off® Contest 42, 2006

Prep Time: 20 Minutes
Start to Finish: 3 Hours

16 bars

CRUST
>>
½ cup Pillsbury Fudge Supreme double chocolate brownie mix (from 15.8-oz box), reserving remaining mix for filling
6 pecan crunch crunchy granola bars (3 pouches from 8.9-oz box), crushed (heaping 1 cup)
¼ cup packed brown sugar
¼ cup chopped pecans or pecan pieces
¼ cup butter or margarine, melted

FILLING
Remaining dry brownie mix
Chocolate Syrup (from mix)
¼ cup vegetable oil
¼ cup water
1 egg or ¼ cup fat-free egg product or 1 egg white

TOPPING
¼ cup packed brown sugar
¼ cup chopped pecans or pecan pieces
¼ cup butter or margarine, melted
¾ cup flaked coconut
¼ teaspoon vanilla

GARNISH, IF DESIRED
Whipped cream or ice cream
Additional crushed pecan crunch crunchy granola bars

1 Bar: Calories 310; Total Fat 17g (Saturated Fat 6g; Trans Fat 0g); Cholesterol 30mg; Sodium 170mg; Total Carbohydrate 38g (Dietary Fiber 1g) **Exchanges:** ½ Starch, 2 Other Carbohydrate, 3½ Fat **Carbohydrate Choices:** 2½

1 Heat oven to 350°F (325°F for dark pan). Spray bottom only of 9- or 8-inch square pan with cooking spray. Set Chocolate Syrup (from brownie mix) aside for filling. In medium bowl, mix crust ingredients. Spread mixture in pan, pressing down evenly with back of spoon or fork.

2 In large bowl, beat filling ingredients 50 strokes with spoon. Spoon and spread batter evenly over crust. In small bowl, mix topping ingredients; sprinkle over filling.

3 Bake 35 to 40 minutes for 9-inch pan (45 to 50 minutes for 8-inch pan) or until coconut is golden brown and bars begin to pull away from sides of pan. Cool 1 hour 30 minutes to 2 hours before serving. For bars, cut into 4 rows by 4 rows. Serve at room temperature topped with whipped cream and additional crushed granola bars.

High Altitude (3500–6500 ft): Do not use 8-inch pan. Stir ¼ cup all-purpose flour into remaining dry brownie mix for filling. Bake 40 to 45 minutes.

take note: To easily crush granola bars, do not unwrap them. Use a rolling pin or smooth side of a meat mallet to crush the bars in the pouches.

caramel chai bars

Kerstin Sinkevicius | Somerville, MA | Bake-Off® Contest 43, 2008

Prep Time: 20 Minutes
Start to Finish: 2 Hours 40 Minutes

16 bars

>> 1 roll (16.5 oz) Pillsbury
    refrigerated sugar cookies
1 package (1.1 oz) chai tea latte
    mix (from 8.8-oz box)
½ cup caramel sundae syrup
2 tablespoons Pillsbury BEST
    all-purpose flour
½ cup ground walnuts

1 Heat oven to 350°F. In large bowl, knead cookie dough and dry chai mix until well blended.

2 Break up ¾ of the chai dough in ungreased 8-inch square pan. Press dough evenly in bottom of pan. (If dough is sticky, use floured fingers.) Bake 12 to 17 minutes or until light golden brown.

3 Meanwhile, in small bowl, mix caramel syrup and flour. In another small bowl, knead remaining ¼ of chai dough and the walnuts.

4 Remove partially baked crust from oven. Gently drizzle caramel mixture evenly over crust. Crumble walnut chai dough evenly over caramel.

5 Bake 22 to 29 minutes longer or until top is golden brown and firm to the touch and caramel is bubbly. Cool completely, about 1 hour 30 minutes. For bars, cut into 4 rows by 4 rows.

High Altitude (3500–6500 ft): In step 2, bake 15 to 20 minutes. In step 5, bake 29 to 32 minutes.

take note: Chai tea latte mix is a blend of black tea, honey, vanilla and spices. You will find it by the tea and coffee in the supermarket.

1 Bar: Calories 190; Total Fat 9g (Saturated Fat 1.5g; Trans Fat 1.5g); Cholesterol 10mg; Sodium 140mg; Total Carbohydrate 27g (Dietary Fiber 0g) **Exchanges:** ½ Starch, 1½ Other Carbohydrate, 1½ Fat **Carbohydrate Choices:** 2

oatmeal carmelitas

Erlyce Larson | Kennedy, MN | Bake-Off® Contest 18, 1967

Prep Time: 30 Minutes
Start to Finish: 2 Hours 55 Minutes

36 bars

CRUST
2 cups Pillsbury BEST all-purpose flour
2 cups quick-cooking oats
1½ cups packed brown sugar
1 teaspoon baking soda
½ teaspoon salt
1¼ cups butter or margarine, softened

FILLING
1 jar (12.25 oz) caramel topping (1 cup)
3 tablespoons Pillsbury BEST all-purpose flour
1 cup semisweet chocolate chips (6 oz)
½ cup chopped nuts

1 Heat oven to 350°F. Spray bottom and sides of 13×9-inch pan with cooking spray. In large bowl, beat crust ingredients with electric mixer on low speed until crumbly. Reserve half of crumb mixture (about 3 cups) for topping. Press remaining crumb mixture in bottom of pan. Bake 10 minutes.

2 Meanwhile, in small bowl, mix caramel topping and 3 tablespoons flour.

3 Remove partially baked crust from oven. Sprinkle chocolate chips and nuts over crust. Drizzle evenly with caramel mixture; sprinkle with reserved crumb mixture.

4 Bake 18 to 22 minutes longer or until golden brown. Cool completely in pan on cooling rack, about 1 hour. Refrigerate 1 to 2 hours or until filling is set. For bars, cut into 6 rows by 6 rows. Store tightly covered.

High Altitude (3500–6500 ft): No change.

1 Bar: Calories 200; Total Fat 9g (Saturated Fat 5g; Trans Fat 0g); Cholesterol 15mg; Sodium 150mg; Total Carbohydrate 27g (Dietary Fiber 1g) **Exchanges:** ½ Starch, 1½ Other Carbohydrate, 1½ Fat **Carbohydrate Choices:** 2

Gretchen Wanek | Oshkosh, WI | Bake-Off® Contest 43, 2008

Prep Time: 20 Minutes
Start to Finish: 4 Hours 25 Minutes

24 bars

>> 1 roll (16.5 oz) Pillsbury
     refrigerated sugar cookies
1 bag (12 oz) semisweet chocolate
     chips (2 cups)
3 cups chopped pecans
½ cup butter or margarine
½ cup packed light brown sugar
1 jar (12.25 oz) caramel topping
     (1 cup)
1 cup graham cracker crumbs
     (16 squares)

1 Heat oven to 350°F (325°F for dark or nonstick pan). Press cookie dough evenly in bottom of ungreased 13×9-inch pan.

2 Sprinkle 1 cup of the chocolate chips and 1½ cups of the pecans over dough; lightly press into dough. Set aside.

3 In 2-quart saucepan, melt butter over medium-high heat. Stir in brown sugar, caramel topping and graham cracker crumbs. Heat to boiling, stirring constantly. Pour over crust in pan; spread evenly. Sprinkle with remaining 1 cup chocolate chips and 1½ cups pecans.

4 Bake 25 to 32 minutes or until edges are deep golden brown and pecans are lightly toasted. Cool on cooling rack 30 minutes; loosen sides from pan, but do not cut. Cool completely, about 3 hours longer. (For firmer bars, let stand an additional 2 hours.) For bars, cut into 6 rows by 4 rows.

High Altitude (3500–6500 ft): Bake 27 to 34 minutes.

1 Bar: Calories 370; Total Fat 22g (Saturated Fat 7g; Trans Fat 1.5g); Cholesterol 15mg; Sodium 160mg; Total Carbohydrate 40g (Dietary Fiber 2g) **Exchanges:** 1 Starch, 1½ Other Carbohydrate, 4½ Fat **Carbohydrate Choices:** 2½

(top left) Rolled Sugar Cookies, page 106; *(top right)* Chocolate Chip–Almond-Cherry Cups, page 92; *(bottom)* Easy Santa Cookies, page 100

holiday cookies and bars

cranberry-orange cookies

Prep Time: 1 Hour
Start to Finish: 1 Hour

About 5 dozen cookies

COOKIES
1½ cups packed brown sugar
1 cup butter or margarine, softened
1 teaspoon vanilla
2 eggs
2¼ cups all-purpose flour
2 teaspoons baking powder
1 teaspoon baking soda
½ teaspoon salt
2 cups old-fashioned or quick-cooking oats
1 cup sweetened dried cranberries
1 cup chopped orange slice candies

GLAZE
¾ cup powdered sugar
2 to 3 teaspoons orange juice

1 Heat oven to 350°F. In large bowl, beat brown sugar and butter with electric mixer on medium speed until light and fluffy. Beat in vanilla and eggs until well blended. On low speed, beat in flour, baking powder, baking soda and salt until well blended. Stir in oats, cranberries and chopped candies.

2 On ungreased cookie sheets, drop dough by rounded teaspoonfuls 2 inches apart.

3 Bake 9 to 11 minutes or until golden brown. Cool 1 minute; remove from cookie sheets to cooling racks. Cool completely, about 15 minutes.

4 In small bowl, mix glaze ingredients, adding enough orange juice until glaze is smooth and thin enough to drizzle. Drizzle glaze over cookies.

High Altitude (3500–6500 ft): No change.

■■■ **take note:** Instant oats should not be used instead of old-fashioned or quick-cooking oats. They are made from precooked and dried sliced oats, which attract moisture and can produce gluey lumps. To easily cut the orange slice candies into pieces, use kitchen scissors sprayed with cooking spray.

1 Cookie: Calories 110; Total Fat 3.5g (Saturated Fat 2g; Trans Fat 0g); Cholesterol 15mg; Sodium 85mg; Total Carbohydrate 19g (Dietary Fiber 0g) **Exchanges:** 1½ Other Carbohydrate, ½ Fat **Carbohydrate Choices:** 1

christmas ornament cookies

Prep Time: 1 Hour
Start to Finish: 1 Hour 30 Minutes

2 dozen cookies

>> 1 roll (16.5 oz) refrigerated sugar
 cookies
¼ cup all-purpose flour
1 egg white, beaten
1 tablespoon red sugar
1 tablespoon green sugar
12 small gumdrops, cut in half

1 In large bowl, break up cookie dough. Stir or knead in flour until well blended. Reshape into 7-inch roll. Cut cookie dough lengthwise into 3 long slices (see Cutting Cookie Dough below). On work surface, separate slices, placing rounded sides down. Lightly brush all cut surfaces with beaten egg white.

2 Sprinkle egg white area of 1 rounded slice with red sugar. Place middle slice on top; sprinkle with green sugar. Place remaining rounded slice, egg white side down, on green sugar; press firmly. If necessary, reshape into roll. Wrap roll in plastic wrap; freeze 30 minutes.

3 Heat oven to 350°F. Cut roll into 24 slices. On ungreased cookie sheets, place slices 1 inch apart.

4 Bake 9 to 11 minutes or until edges are light golden brown. Immediately press gumdrop half onto outer edge of each cookie to look like ornament hanger; remove from cookie sheets to cooling racks.

High Altitude (3500–6500 ft): Bake 12 to 14 minutes.

take note: Be sure to use a sharp, long, thin-bladed knife to cut the cookie dough roll into slices.

Cutting Cookie Dough

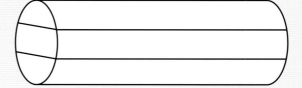

1 Cookie: Calories 100; Total Fat 4g (Saturated Fat 1g; Trans Fat 1g); Cholesterol 5mg; Sodium 65mg; Total Carbohydrate 16g (Dietary Fiber 0g) **Exchanges:** 1 Other Carbohydrate, 1 Fat **Carbohydrate Choices:** 1

chocolate chip–almond-cherry cups

Prep Time: 1 Hour 10 Minutes
Start to Finish: 1 Hour 55 Minutes

4 dozen cookies

COOKIE CUPS
>> 1 roll (16.5 oz) refrigerated
   chocolate chip cookies
½ cup almond paste, crumbled
½ cup dried cherries
½ cup cherry preserves

ICING
1 cup powdered sugar
¼ teaspoon almond extract
4 to 5 teaspoons milk
Additional powdered sugar,
   if desired

1 Heat oven to 350°F. Spray 48 miniature muffin cups with baking spray with flour. In large bowl, break up cookie dough. With hands, knead in almond paste and cherries.

2 Divide dough into 48 pieces. Shape each piece into ball; place in muffin cup. With thumb, make indentation in center of each.

3 Bake 6 to 8 minutes or until edges are golden brown. Cool in pan on cooling rack 5 minutes. Run knife around edge of cookies to loosen; cool 1 to 2 minutes longer. Remove from muffin cups; place on cooling racks to cool completely.

4 Spoon ½ teaspoon preserves into each cooled cup.

5 In small bowl, mix 1 cup powdered sugar, the almond extract and enough milk until icing is smooth and thin enough to drizzle. Drizzle over cookies. Let stand about 30 minutes or until set. Sprinkle with additional powdered sugar.

High Altitude (3500–6500 ft): Bake 10 to 12 minutes.

Chocolate Chip–Cranberry-Orange Cups: Substitute ½ cup sweetened dried cranberries for the cherries and ½ cup orange marmalade for the cherry preserves.

■■■ **take note:** You'll find the almond paste in tubes with the other baking ingredients at the grocery store. Check the date on the package for freshness. Fresh almond paste should be slightly soft.

1 Cookie: Calories 80; Total Fat 3g (Saturated Fat 0.5g; Trans Fat 0.5g); Cholesterol 0mg; Sodium 30mg; Total Carbohydrate 13g (Dietary Fiber 0g) **Exchanges:** 1 Other Carbohydrate, ½ Fat **Carbohydrate Choices:** 1

holiday moments

Prep Time: 1 Hour
Start to Finish: 2 Hours

About 3 dozen cookies

1 cup butter or margarine,
   softened
¾ cup cornstarch
⅓ cup powdered sugar
1 cup all-purpose flour
3 tablespoons powdered sugar
2 tablespoons red sugar
2 tablespoons green sugar

1 In large bowl, beat butter with electric mixer on medium speed until light and fluffy. On low speed, beat in cornstarch and ⅓ cup powdered sugar until moistened. Beat on high speed until light and fluffy. On low speed, beat in flour until dough forms. Cover with plastic wrap; refrigerate at least 1 hour for easier handling.

2 Heat oven to 350°F. Shape dough into 1-inch balls. On ungreased cookie sheets, place balls 1 inch apart.

3 Bake 9 to 15 minutes or until cookies are very light golden brown. Cool 1 minute; remove from cookie sheets to cooling racks.

4 In small bowl, mix 3 tablespoons powdered sugar, the red sugar and green sugar. Carefully roll warm cookies in sugar mixture.

High Altitude (3500–6500 ft): Increase flour to 1¼ cups.

■■■ **take note:** Cornstarch gives the cookie dough structure while ensuring that the cookies will be extra light and tender. Be sure the cookies are still warm when rolling in the sugar mixture. The butter in the cookies will still be soft, helping the sugar stick to the cookies.

1 Cookie: Calories 80; Total Fat 5g (Saturated Fat 3.5g; Trans Fat 0g); Cholesterol 15mg; Sodium 35mg; Total Carbohydrate 8g (Dietary Fiber 0g) **Exchanges:** ½ Other Carbohydrate, 1 Fat **Carbohydrate Choices:** ½

spritz cookies

Prep Time: 50 Minutes
Start to Finish: 50 Minutes

About 5 dozen cookies

1 cup powdered sugar
1 cup butter,* softened
½ teaspoon vanilla
1 egg
2⅓ cups all-purpose flour
¼ teaspoon salt

1 Heat oven to 400°F. In large bowl, beat powdered sugar, butter, vanilla and egg with electric mixer on medium speed until light and fluffy. On low speed, beat in flour and salt until well blended.

2 Fit cookie press with desired template. Fill cookie press with dough. On ungreased cookie sheets, press dough to form cookies.

3 Bake 5 to 7 minutes or until edges are firm but not brown. Immediately remove from cookie sheets to cooling racks.

High Altitude (3500–6500 ft): No change.

*We recommend using only butter for the best flavor.

Chocolate Spritz Cookies: Melt and cool 2 oz unsweetened baking chocolate; add to the powdered sugar mixture.

Eggnog Spritz Cookies: Substitute 1 teaspoon rum extract for the vanilla, and add ¼ teaspoon ground nutmeg with the flour.

Orange Spritz Cookies: Add 1 tablespoon grated orange peel with the flour.

1 Cookie: Calories 50; Total Fat 3g (Saturated Fat 2g; Trans Fat 0g); Cholesterol 10mg; Sodium 35mg; Total Carbohydrate 6g (Dietary Fiber 0g) **Exchanges:** ½ Other Carbohydrate, ½ Fat **Carbohydrate Choices:** ½

peppermint spritz candy canes

Prep Time: 50 Minutes
Start to Finish: 50 Minutes

About 4 dozen cookies

>> **1 roll (16.5 oz) refrigerated sugar cookies**
¼ cup all-purpose flour
¼ to ½ teaspoon peppermint extract
Red sugar

1 Heat oven to 350°F. In medium bowl, break up cookie dough. Stir or knead in flour until blended. Add peppermint extract; stir or knead dough until well blended.

2 Fit cookie press with star template. Place about half of dough in cookie press. On ungreased cookie sheets, press dough into 5-inch strips. With fingers, shape top of each strips to resemble candy cane. Sprinkle with red sugar. Repeat with remaining half of dough.

3 Bake 5 to 7 minutes or until edges are light golden brown. Immediately remove from cookie sheets to cooling racks.

High Altitude (3500–6500 ft): Bake 7 to 9 minutes.

take note: To give the cookies the traditional peppermint stick flavor, be sure to use extract labeled "peppermint," not "mint" or "spearmint."

1 Cookie: Calories 50; Total Fat 2g (Saturated Fat 0.5g; Trans Fat 0.5g); Cholesterol 0mg; Sodium 30mg; Total Carbohydrate 7g (Dietary Fiber 0g) **Exchanges:** ½ Other Carbohydrate, ½ Fat **Carbohydrate Choices:** ½

rosettes

Prep Time: 1 Hour 10 Minutes
Start to Finish: 1 Hour 10 Minutes

About 4½ dozen rosettes

2 eggs
1 tablespoon granulated sugar
¼ teaspoon salt
1 cup all-purpose flour
1 cup milk
¼ teaspoon vanilla
Oil for deep frying
Powdered sugar, if desired

1 In small bowl, beat eggs slightly. Beat in sugar and salt. Alternately beat in flour, ¼ cup at a time, and milk, ¼ cup at a time, until smooth. Stir in vanilla.

2 In deep fryer or heavy saucepan, heat 3 to 4 inches oil to 375°F. Place rosette iron in hot oil for about 30 to 60 seconds or until iron is hot. Gently dip hot iron into batter; DO NOT ALLOW BATTER TO RUN OVER TOP OF IRON.

3 Return iron to hot oil, immersing completely for 25 to 30 seconds or until rosette is crisp and lightly browned. (If rosettes drop from the mold, the oil is too hot. If rosettes are soft, increase cooking time.) Remove from oil; allow oil to drip off. Gently slip rosette off iron onto paper towel. Repeat for remaining cookies.

4 Cool completely. Sprinkle with powdered sugar. Store in tightly covered container. If powdered sugar dissolves, sprinkle again before serving.

High Altitude (3500–6500 ft): No change.

Iced Nutmeg Rosettes: Add ½ teaspoon ground nutmeg with the sugar. In small bowl, mix 1 cup powdered sugar, ½ teaspoon vanilla and enough milk for desired dipping consistency; stir until smooth. Gently dip top edges of rosettes (not rounded bottoms) into icing. Sprinkle with nutmeg. Let dry. Store in tightly covered container, making sure sides do not touch.

▪▪▪ **take note:** If the rosettes have blisters, the eggs have been beaten too much. They may not look as perfect as you like but they will still taste great.

1 Rosette: Calories 40; Total Fat 3.5g (Saturated Fat 0.5g; Trans Fat 0g); Cholesterol 10mg; Sodium 15mg; Total Carbohydrate 2g (Dietary Fiber 0g) **Exchanges:** 1 Fat **Carbohydrate Choices:** 0

pistachio shortbread

Prep Time: 30 Minutes
Start to Finish: 1 Hour 15 Minutes

32 cookies

COOKIES
1 cup butter or margarine, softened
½ cup granulated sugar
½ cup finely chopped pistachio nuts
2¼ cups all-purpose flour
1 teaspoon vanilla

ICING
1 cup powdered sugar
1 to 3 tablespoons milk

1 Heat oven to 325°F. Spray 2 cookie sheets with cooking spray.

2 In large bowl, beat butter and granulated sugar with electric mixer on medium speed until light and fluffy. Reserve 2 tablespoons of the nuts. On low speed, beat in remaining nuts, flour and vanilla until well blended. Dough will be stiff.

3 Divide dough evenly into 4 pieces; shape each piece into a ball. On lightly floured surface, pat each ball to form 6-inch round. Transfer rounds to cookie sheets, using 2 large pancake turners. With table knife, lightly make indentations on surface of dough, dividing each round into 8 wedges.

4 Bake 16 to 21 minutes or until edges are light golden brown. Cool 2 minutes; remove from cookie sheets. Cut each round into 8 wedges; place on cooling racks. Cool completely, about 15 minutes.

5 Very finely chop reserved 2 tablespoons nuts. In small bowl, mix icing ingredients, adding enough milk until smooth and thick enough to drizzle. Drizzle icing in zigzag design over each cookie. Before icing sets, sprinkle cookies with nuts.

High Altitude (3500–6500 ft): No change.

Pistachio Shortbread Trees: Prepare and shape dough as directed. After scoring each round into 8 wedges, insert half a pretzel twist or stick in outside edge of each wedge for tree truck. Bake and decorate as directed.

■■■ **take note:** Pistachio nuts are easy to shell because the shells open naturally when the nuts are ripe. Discard unopened pistachio nuts because they are not ripe. Shelled pistachio nuts are more expensive, but they save prep time.

1 Cookie: Calories 120; Total Fat 7g (Saturated Fat 4g; Trans Fat 0g); Cholesterol 15mg; Sodium 40mg; Total Carbohydrate 14g (Dietary Fiber 0g) **Exchanges:** 1 Other Carbohydrate, 1½ Fat **Carbohydrate Choices:** 1

easy santa cookies

Prep Time: 1 Hour
Start to Finish: 2 Hours

34 cookies

COOKIES
>> 1 roll (16.5 oz) refrigerated sugar
   cookies
¼ cup all-purpose flour

ICING
2 cups powdered sugar
2 tablespoons butter or
   margarine, softened
2 to 3 tablespoons milk
2 to 3 drops red food color

DECORATION
68 semisweet chocolate chips
   (about ¼ cup)
34 red cinnamon candies
⅔ cup coconut
34 miniature marshmallows

1. In large bowl, break up cookie dough. Stir or knead in flour until well blended. Reshape into 7-inch roll. If too soft to cut into slices, refrigerate up to 30 minutes.

2. Heat oven to 350°F. Cut dough into 34 slices. On ungreased cookie sheets, place slices 3 inches apart.

3. Bake 8 to 12 minutes or until golden brown. Cool 2 minutes; remove from cookie sheets to cooling racks. Cool completely, about 5 minutes.

4. In small bowl, beat powdered sugar, butter and enough milk until smooth and spreadable. Place about ⅓ of the frosting in another small bowl; stir in food color until blended. Place about ⅓ cup remaining white frosting in small resealable food-storage plastic bag; seal bag. Cut small tip from bottom corner of bag; set aside.

5. Frost top third of each cookie with red frosting. Frost bottom third with white frosting. Use small amount of frosting to attach chocolate chips for eyes and cinnamon candy for nose. Gently press coconut into white frosting for beard. Press marshmallow into red frosting for tassel on cap. With frosting in bag, pipe brim on hat. Let cookies stand about 30 minutes until frosting is set.

High Altitude (3500–6500 ft): No change.

■■■ **take note:** You can substitute paste food color, but use a small amount because it produces an intense, deep color. Paste colors can be found at baking-supply stores and craft stores with the cake-decorating supplies.

1 Cookie: Calories 120; Total Fat 4.5g (Saturated Fat 2g; Trans Fat 0.5g); Cholesterol 5mg; Sodium 55mg; Total Carbohydrate 19g (Dietary Fiber 0g) **Exchanges:** 1 Other Carbohydrate, 1 Fat **Carbohydrate Choices:** 1

macaroon-topped sugar cookies

Prep Time: 45 Minutes
Start to Finish: 1 Hour 15 Minutes

32 cookies

›› **1 roll (16.5 oz) refrigerated sugar cookies**
¼ cup all-purpose flour
1½ cups coconut
⅓ cup sugar
1 tablespoon all-purpose flour
¼ teaspoon almond extract
1 egg white
16 red or green maraschino cherries, halved, drained on paper towel

1 Cookie: Calories 100; Total Fat 4.5g (Saturated Fat 2g; Trans Fat 1g); Cholesterol 5mg; Sodium 60mg; Total Carbohydrate 15g (Dietary Fiber 0g) **Exchanges:** 1 Other Carbohydrate, 1 Fat **Carbohydrate Choices:** 1

1 In large bowl, break up cookie dough. Stir or knead in ¼ cup flour until well blended. Reshape into 7-inch roll. If dough is too soft to cut into slices, refrigerate up to 30 minutes.

2 Heat oven to 350°F. In medium bowl, mix coconut, sugar, 1 tablespoon flour, the almond extract and egg white until well blended.

3 Cut cookie dough into 32 slices. On ungreased cookie sheets, place slices 2 inches apart. On each slice, spoon 1 rounded teaspoon coconut mixture, spreading slightly. Press 1 cherry half, cut side down, on each.

4 Bake 12 to 15 minutes or until edges are light golden brown. Cool 1 minute; remove from cookie sheets to cooling racks.

High Altitude (3500–6500 ft): After adding flour to cookie dough and reshaping into 8-inch roll, freeze dough 30 minutes.

■■■ **take note:** If you don't get the cookies off the cookie sheet in time and they start to stick, pop the cookie sheet back in the hot oven for a minute or two. The heat should soften the cookies slightly, making removal easier.

more holiday cookies and bars

peppermint pinwheel cookies

Prep Time: 1 Hour 30 Minutes
Start to Finish: 10 Hours 30 Minutes

About 10 dozen cookies

3 cups all-purpose flour
½ teaspoon baking soda
¼ teaspoon salt
1 cup sugar
1 cup butter or margarine, softened
2 tablespoons milk
1 teaspoon vanilla
1 egg
½ teaspoon peppermint extract
4 or 5 drops red food color
¼ cup pink sugar

1 In medium bowl, mix flour, baking soda and salt; set aside. In large bowl, beat sugar, butter, milk, vanilla and egg with electric mixer on medium speed until light and fluffy. On low speed, beat in flour mixture until well blended.

2 Place half of dough in food-storage plastic bag or wrap in plastic wrap. To remaining half of dough, add peppermint extract and food color; mix well. Place pink dough in plastic bag or wrap in plastic wrap. Refrigerate both portions of dough 1 hour.

3 Divide each portion of dough in half. Place 1 part white dough between 2 pieces of plastic wrap; roll into 10×8-inch rectangle, using rolling pin. Repeat with 1 part pink dough. Remove top sheets of plastic wrap from white and pink dough. Place pink dough over white dough; remove plastic wrap from pink dough. Trim edges, if desired. Starting at 10-inch edge, roll up both layers of dough, removing plastic wrap from bottom as dough is rolled. Repeat with remaining dough to form second roll.

4 Place 2 tablespoons of the pink sugar on separate sheet of plastic wrap. Roll 1 roll of dough in pink sugar, pressing gently into dough. Repeat with second roll. Wrap rolls in plastic wrap; refrigerate 8 hours or until firm.

5 Heat oven to 375°F. Cut dough into ⅛-inch slices. On ungreased cookie sheets, place slices 1 inch apart.

6 Bake 5 to 7 minutes or until light golden brown. Cool 1 minute; remove from cookie sheets to cooling racks.

High Altitude (3500–6500 ft): No change.

Orange Swirl Cookies: Substitute orange extract for the peppermint extract and red and yellow food colors for red food color.

Heart Swirl Cookies: To make heart-shaped cookies, gently shape each roll of pink and white layers of dough into a heart shape. Omit rolling in pink sugar. Cut rolls into slices and bake.

1 Cookie: Calories 35; Total Fat 1.5g (Saturated Fat 1g; Trans Fat 0g); Cholesterol 5mg; Sodium 20mg; Total Carbohydrate 4g (Dietary Fiber 0g) **Exchanges:** ½ Other Carbohydrate **Carbohydrate Choices:** 0

rugelach

Prep Time: 1 Hour 25 Minutes
Start to Finish: 2 Hours 55 Minutes

64 cookies

1 cup butter or margarine,
   softened
2 tablespoons granulated sugar
1 package (8 oz) cream cheese,
   softened
2 cups all-purpose flour
½ cup finely chopped dates
½ cup finely chopped pistachio
   nuts or almonds
⅓ cup granulated sugar
¼ cup butter or margarine,
   softened
2 teaspoons ground cinnamon
1 tablespoon powdered sugar

1 In large bowl, beat 1 cup butter, 2 tablespoons granulated sugar and the cream cheese with electric mixer on medium speed until light and fluffy. On low speed, beat in flour until well blended. Shape dough into ball; divide into 4 pieces. Shape each piece into ball; flatten into ½-inch-thick disk. Wrap each disk in plastic wrap; refrigerate about 2 hours for easier handling.

2 Heat oven to 375°F. Spray 2 cookie sheets with cooking spray. In small bowl, mix dates, nuts, ⅓ cup granulated sugar, ¼ cup butter and the cinnamon.

3 On floured surface, roll 1 disk of dough at a time to ⅛-inch thickness into 12-inch round, using lightly floured rolling pin. (Keep remaining disks of dough refrigerated.) Sprinkle ¼ of date-nut mixture onto round; press into dough slightly. Cut round into 16 wedges. Roll up each wedge from curved edge to point. Place on cookie sheets.

4 Bake 13 to 18 minutes or until light golden brown. Immediately remove from cookie sheets to cooling racks. Cool completely, about 30 minutes. Sprinkle with powdered sugar.

High Altitude (3500–6500 ft): No change.

take note: A Hanukkah tradition, these tender crescent-shaped cookies are filled with a nut-cinnamon mixture. Arrange rugelach evenly on the cookie sheets. Avoid crowding, or the middle cookies will not be done when the cookies along the edges are ready.

1 Cookie: Calories 80; Total Fat 5g (Saturated Fat 3g; Trans Fat 0g); Cholesterol 15mg; Sodium 35mg; Total Carbohydrate 6g (Dietary Fiber 0g) **Exchanges:** ½ Starch, 1 Fat **Carbohydrate Choices:** ½

rolled sugar cookies

Prep Time: 1 Hour 30 Minutes
Start to Finish: 2 Hours 30 Minutes

About 6 dozen cookies

COOKIES
1 cup granulated sugar
1 cup butter or margarine,
   softened
3 tablespoons milk
1 teaspoon vanilla
1 egg
3 cups all-purpose flour
1½ teaspoons baking powder
½ teaspoon salt
Granulated or colored sugars,
   candy sprinkles and small
   candy decors, if desired

GLAZE, IF DESIRED
1½ cups powdered sugar
3 to 3½ tablespoons milk

1 In large bowl, mix 1 cup granulated sugar, the butter, milk, vanilla and egg until well blended. Stir in flour, baking powder and salt until mixed. Cover with plastic wrap; refrigerate 1 hour for easier handling.

2 Heat oven to 400°F. On lightly floured surface, roll ⅓ of dough at a time to ⅛-inch thickness, using lightly floured rolling pin. (Keep remaining dough refrigerated.) Cut dough with floured 2-inch cookie cutter in desired shape. On ungreased cookie sheets, place cutouts 1 inch apart. If not using glaze, sprinkle with sugar.

3 Bake 5 to 9 minutes or until edges are light golden brown. Immediately remove from cookie sheets to cooling racks. Cool completely, about 15 minutes.

4 In small bowl, mix powdered sugar and enough milk until smooth and spreadable. Spread glaze over cookies. Sprinkle with colored sugar or decorate as desired.

High Altitude (3500–6500 ft): No change.

Painted Sugar Cookies: Omit sugars, candy sprinkles and small candy decors. Divide 1½ cups evaporated milk among small bowls; tint each with a different food color. Using clean small paintbrush and colored milk, paint desired designs on unbaked cookies. Bake as directed.

■■■ **take note:** If some of your cutout cookies are thicker than the others, don't reroll the dough. Instead, place the thinner ones in the center of the cookie sheet and the thicker ones around the edges to get more even browning.

1 Cookie (without Glaze): Calories 50; Total Fat 2.5g (Saturated Fat 1.5g; Trans Fat 0g); Cholesterol 10mg; Sodium 45mg; Total Carbohydrate 7g (Dietary Fiber 0g) **Exchanges:** ½ Other Carbohydrate, ½ Fat **Carbohydrate Choices:** ½

cream cheese sugar cookies

Prep Time: 1 Hour
Start to Finish: 1 Hour

About 6 dozen cookies

1 cup granulated sugar
1 cup butter or margarine,
    softened
1 package (3 oz) cream cheese,
    softened
½ teaspoon salt
½ teaspoon almond extract
½ teaspoon vanilla
1 egg yolk
2 cups all-purpose flour
Colored sugar or candy sprinkles,
    if desired

1 In large bowl, beat all ingredients except flour and colored sugar with electric mixer on medium speed until light and fluffy. On low speed, beat in flour until well blended.

2 Shape dough into 3 disks. Wrap each disk in plastic wrap; refrigerate 1 hour for easier handling.

3 Heat oven to 375°F. On floured surface, roll 1 disk of dough at a time to ⅛-inch thickness, using lightly floured rolling pin. (Keep remaining dough refrigerated.) Cut dough with lightly floured 2½-inch round or desired shape cookie cutter. On ungreased cookie sheets, place cutouts 1 inch apart. Decorate with colored sugar or candy sprinkles.

4 Bake 6 to 10 minutes or until light golden brown. Immediately remove from cookie sheets to cooling racks.

High Altitude (3500–6500 ft): Increase flour to 2¼ cups.

Tri-Cornered Cream Cheese Sugar Cookies: Prepare and roll dough as directed. Cut with floured 2½-inch round cookie cutter. Place 1 inch apart on ungreased cookie sheets. Spoon 1 teaspoon jam or jelly on center of each round. To shape triangles, fold 3 sides in without covering jam; pinch corners to seal. Bake as directed. Sprinkle with powdered sugar.

■■■ **take note:** If you prefer frosted sugar cookies, mix 3 cups powdered sugar, ⅓ cup softened butter or margarine and 1½ teaspoons vanilla until smooth. Stir in 1 tablespoon milk, then add additional milk until the frosting is smooth and spreadable.

1 Cookie: Calories 50; Total Fat 3g (Saturated Fat 2g; Trans Fat 0g); Cholesterol 10mg; Sodium 40mg; Total Carbohydrate 5g (Dietary Fiber 0g) **Exchanges:** ½ Other Carbohydrate, ½ Fat **Carbohydrate Choices:** ½

No Cookie Cutters?

Want to make rolled-out cookies but have no cookie cutters? Use items you may have around the kitchen. To help prevent sticking, spray the cutting edge with cooking spray or dip in flour before using.

Crimper: Cut dough into squares, rectangles or triangles with a scalloped edge.

Jar or Bottle Lid: Roll cookie dough ¼ inch thick, or less, so the lid cuts through the dough. Lids with a thinner edge are easiest to use.

Can: Remove both ends of the can before washing. Be sure one end has a rolled edge to prevent cutting hands when cutting dough. Shorter cans are the easiest to use.

Drinking Glass: Select a thinner glass so cutting the dough will be easier.

Pizza Wheel: Cut dough easily into squares, rectangles or triangles with straight edges.

gingerbread people

Prep Time: 1 Hour 15 Minutes
Start to Finish: 2 Hours 15 Minutes

About 3 dozen cookies

COOKIES
1 cup shortening
1 cup molasses
3 cups all-purpose flour
2 teaspoons baking soda
1 teaspoon salt
½ teaspoon ground ginger
¼ teaspoon ground nutmeg
¼ teaspoon ground cloves

FROSTING
6 cups powdered sugar
6 tablespoons butter or
  margarine, softened
1½ teaspoons vanilla
⅓ to ½ cup milk
Food color, if desired
Colored sugar and candies,
  if desired

1 In large bowl, beat shortening and molasses with electric mixer on medium speed until well blended. On low speed, beat in remaining cookie ingredients until well blended. Cover with plastic wrap; refrigerate at least 1 hour for easier handling.

2 Heat oven to 350°F. On well-floured surface, roll half of dough at a time to ¼-inch thickness, using lightly floured rolling pin. (Keep remaining dough refrigerated.) Cut dough with floured 5×3-inch gingerbread boy or girl cookie cutters or other shaped cutters. On ungreased cookie sheets, place cutouts 1 inch apart.

3 Bake 8 to 10 minutes or until set. Cool 1 minute; remove from cookie sheets to cooling racks. Cool completely, about 15 minutes.

4 Meanwhile, in large bowl, beat powdered sugar, butter, vanilla and enough milk for desired spreading or piping consistency until smooth. If desired, remove half the frosting and divide among small bowls; add a different food color to each bowl. Frost cookies with white frosting and pipe with colored frostings to decorate. Decorated with colored sugar and candies.

High Altitude (3500–6500 ft): Decrease molasses to ⅔ cup. Increase flour to 3¼ cups.

Stenciled Gingerbread Hearts: Omit frosting. After rolling dough, cut with floured 2 ½- to 3-inch heart-shaped cookie cutter. Bake and cool as directed. Brush cooled cookies lightly with milk. Place a lacy paper doily or stencil design on cookie; press down. Using wire strainer, sprinkle powdered sugar evenly over holes in doily; carefully remove doily. Let dry completely.

■■■ **take note:** If you use cookie cutters smaller or larger than the suggested 5-inch cutter, be sure to adjust the baking time by either checking a minute or two before the minimum time for smaller cookies or adding time for larger ones.

1 Cookie: Calories 220; Total Fat 8g (Saturated Fat 2.5g; Trans Fat 1g); Cholesterol 5mg; Sodium 150mg; Total Carbohydrate 35g (Dietary Fiber 0g) **Exchanges:** ½ Starch, 2 Other Carbohydrate, 1½ Fat **Carbohydrate Choices:** 2

stained-glass christmas cookies

Prep Time: 2 Hours 45 Minutes
Start to Finish: 3 Hours

About 3 dozen cookies

About 15 brightly colored
  hard candies (ring-shaped,
  rectangular or round)
1 cup butter or margarine,
  softened
⅔ cup sugar
½ cup light corn syrup
2 teaspoons vanilla
¼ teaspoon lemon extract,
  if desired
3 cups all-purpose flour
¾ teaspoon baking powder
½ teaspoon salt

1 Heat oven to 350°F. Line cookie sheets with cooking parchment paper. Place each color candy in separate resealable freezer plastic bag; seal bag. Coarsely crush candy, using rolling pin; set aside.

2 In large bowl, beat butter and sugar with electric mixer on medium speed until light and fluffy. Beat in corn syrup, vanilla and lemon extract. On low speed, gradually beat in flour, baking powder and salt.

3 Divide dough in half. On floured surface, roll each half to ¼-inch thickness, using lightly floured rolling pin. Cut dough with floured 3-inch cookie cutter. Cut out and remove several smaller dough shapes from each cookie. Place cookies 2 inches apart on cookie sheets. If desired, reroll small cutouts with remaining dough. Fill each hole in cookies with about ½ teaspoon crushed candy.

4 Bake 8 to 10 minutes or until edges are light golden brown and candy is melted. Place cookie sheets on cooling racks; cool cookies 8 minutes. With metal pancake turner, gently lift warm cookies from parchment paper; place on cooling racks. Cool completely, about 15 minutes. Store in loosely covered containers so the candy doesn't soften or become cloudy.

High Altitude (3500–6500 ft): No change.

Stained-Glass Christmas Cookie Ornaments: Cut a ¼-inch hole, using the end of a straw, in the top of each cookie before baking. To make a loop to hang baked cookies, insert a piece of ribbon or cord through the hole and tie the ends together.

take note: For the "stained glass," cut out shapes such as circles, hearts or holiday shapes with small cookie cutters or canapé cutters found in specialty food stores.

1 Cookie: Calories 120; Total Fat 5g (Saturated Fat 3.5g; Trans Fat 0g); Cholesterol 15mg; Sodium 85mg; Total Carbohydrate 18g (Dietary Fiber 0g) **Exchanges:** ½ Starch, ½ Other Carbohydrate, 1 Fat **Carbohydrate Choices:** 1

linzer sandwich cookies

Prep Time: 1 Hour
Start to Finish: 4 Hours

About 26 sandwich cookies

¾ cup hazelnuts (filberts)
½ cup packed light brown sugar
2½ cups all-purpose flour
2 teaspoons cream of tartar
1 teaspoon baking soda
½ teaspoon salt
¼ teaspoon ground cinnamon
1 cup butter or margarine,
    softened
1 egg
1 teaspoon vanilla
Powdered sugar, if desired
½ cup seedless raspberry jam

1. Heat oven to 350°F. Spread hazelnuts in ungreased shallow baking pan. Bake uncovered about 6 minutes, stirring occasionally. Rub nuts in a kitchen towel to remove loose skins (some skins may not come off); cool 5 to 10 minutes. Turn off oven.

2. In food processor bowl with metal blade, place nuts and ¼ cup of the brown sugar. Cover; process with about 10 on-and-off pulses, 2 to 3 seconds each, until nuts are finely ground but not oily.

3. In small bowl, mix flour, cream of tartar, baking soda, salt and cinnamon; set aside.

4. In large bowl, beat butter and remaining ¼ cup brown sugar with electric mixer on medium speed about 3 minutes or until smooth. Add nut mixture; beat about 1 minute or until mixed. Beat in egg and vanilla. With spoon, stir in flour mixture about 1 minute or just until blended. Shape dough into 2 balls; flatten each ball into a disk. Wrap each disk separately in plastic wrap; refrigerate at least 2 hours until firm.

5. Heat oven to 425°F. Remove 1 disk of dough from refrigerator. On well-floured surface, roll dough to ⅛-inch thickness, using lightly floured rolling pin. Cut dough with 2½-inch cookie cutter in desired shape. On ungreased cookie sheets, place cutouts about 1 inch apart.

6. Roll and cut other half of dough. Using a 1-inch square or round cutter, cut out the center of half of the cookies. Reroll dough centers and cut out more cookies.

7. Bake 4 to 5 minutes or until edges are light golden brown. Remove from cookie sheets to cooling racks. Cool about 10 minutes.

8. Lightly sprinkle powdered sugar over cookies with center cutouts. Spread about 1 teaspoon raspberry jam over bottom side of each whole cookie. Top with a cutout cookie. Cool completely, about 1 hour. (Or instead of sprinkling with powdered sugar, cool cookies completely. Make a glaze by mixing ¾ cup powdered sugar and 2 to 3 teaspoons milk; drizzle glaze over tops of sandwich cookies and sprinkle with colored sugars or decors.)

High Altitude (3500–6500 ft): No change.

1 Sandwich Cookie: Calories 170; Total Fat 10g (Saturated Fat 4.5g; Trans Fat 0g); Cholesterol 25mg; Sodium 150mg; Total Carbohydrate 18g (Dietary Fiber 0g) **Exchanges:** ½ Starch, ½ Other Carbohydrate, 2 Fat **Carbohydrate Choices:** 1

two-in-one holiday bars

Prep Time: 20 Minutes
Start to Finish: 1 Hour 50 Minutes

48 bars

BARS
1 cup granulated sugar
¾ cup butter or margarine,
    softened
1 teaspoon vanilla
1 egg
2 cups all-purpose flour
1 cup diced mixed candied fruit
½ cup semisweet chocolate chips
½ cup chopped pecans

GLAZE
1 cup powdered sugar
1 to 2 tablespoons milk

1 Heat oven to 350°F. In large bowl, beat granulated sugar and butter with electric mixer on medium speed until light and fluffy. Beat in vanilla and egg. On low speed, beat in flour until well blended. Spread dough in ungreased 15×10×1-inch pan.

2 Sprinkle candied fruit over half of dough. Sprinkle chocolate chips and pecans over other half of dough. Press lightly into dough.

3 Bake 25 to 30 minutes or until edges are light golden brown. Cool completely, about 1 hour.

4 In small bowl, mix powdered sugar and enough milk until smooth and thin enough to drizzle. Drizzle glaze over bars. Let stand until glaze is set. For bars, cut into 8 rows by 6 rows.

High Altitude (3500–6500 ft): Increase flour to 2¼ cups.

Two-in-One Cherry Holiday Bars: Substitute ½ cup chopped red candied cherries and ½ cup green candied cherries for the mixed candied fruit.

■■■ **take note:** You can create your own combination of toppings for these bars. Use red and green candy-coated chocolate candies or vanilla chips for the chocolate chips. Or walnuts, peanuts or pistachios for the pecans.

1 Bar: Calories 100; Total Fat 4.5g (Saturated Fat 2.5g; Trans Fat 0g); Cholesterol 10mg; Sodium 25mg; Total Carbohydrate 14g (Dietary Fiber 0g) **Exchanges:** 1 Other Carbohydrate, 1 Fat **Carbohydrate Choices:** 1

raspberry cheesecake bars

Prep Time: 20 Minutes
Start to Finish: 1 Hour 55 Minutes

25 bars

CRUST
½ **cup sugar**
½ **cup butter or margarine,**
   softened
1¼ **cups all-purpose flour**

FILLING
1 **package (8 oz) cream cheese,**
   softened
½ **cup sugar**
½ **teaspoon almond extract**
1 **egg**

TOPPING
4 **tablespoons seedless red**
   raspberry jam

1 Heat oven to 350°F. Spray bottom and sides of 9-inch square pan with cooking spray. In large bowl, mix ½ cup sugar and the butter until well blended. Stir in flour until crumbly. Press mixture in bottom of pan.

2 Bake 15 to 18 minutes or until edges are light golden brown. Meanwhile, in large bowl, beat filling ingredients with electric mixer on medium speed until well blended.

3 Remove partially baked crust from oven. Pour filling over crust. In small bowl, stir 2 tablespoons of the jam until softened; spoon over cream cheese mixture. With tip of spoon, carefully swirl jam into top of filling (do not disturb crust).

4 Bake 15 to 20 minutes longer or until filling is set. Cool 30 minutes.

5 Stir remaining 2 tablespoons jam until smooth; spread evenly over cooled bars. Refrigerate 30 minutes. For bars, cut into 5 rows by 5 rows. Store in refrigerator.

High Altitude (3500–6500 ft): In step 2, bake 18 to 21 minutes.

Strawberry Cheesecake Bars: Substitute ½ teaspoon vanilla for the almond extract and 4 tablespoons seedless strawberry jam for the raspberry jam.

▪▪▪ **take note:** To make it easier to spread the jam over the bars, melt the jam slightly in the microwave. Place the jam in a microwavable dish, and microwave on High 10 to 15 seconds or just until it's warm.

1 Bar: Calories 130; Total Fat 7g (Saturated Fat 4.5g; Trans Fat 0g); Cholesterol 30mg; Sodium 55mg; Total Carbohydrate 15g (Dietary Fiber 0g) **Exchanges:** 1 Other Carbohydrate, 1½ Fat **Carbohydrate Choices:** 1

scandinavian almond bars

Prep Time: 10 Minutes
Start to Finish: 1 Hour 5 Minutes

48 bars

>> **1 roll (16.5 oz) refrigerated sugar cookies**
½ teaspoon ground cinnamon
1 teaspoon almond extract
1 egg white
1 tablespoon water
1 cup sliced almonds
¼ cup sugar

1 Heat oven to 350°F. Spray bottom and sides of 15×10×1-inch pan with cooking spray.

2 In large bowl, break up cookie dough. Stir or knead in cinnamon and almond extract until well blended. With floured fingers, press dough mixture evenly in bottom of pan to form crust.

3 In small bowl, beat egg white and water until frothy. Brush over dough. Sprinkle evenly with almonds and sugar.

4 Bake 17 to 22 minutes or until edges are light golden brown. Cool completely, about 30 minutes. For diamond-shaped bars, cut 5 straight parallel lines about 1½ inches apart down length of pan; cut diagonal lines about 1½ inches apart across straight lines.

High Altitude (3500–6500 ft): No change.

■■■ **take note:** If you prefer square bars rather than diagonally shaped ones, cut into 8 rows by 6 rows. Store these bars tightly covered at room temperature.

1 Bar: Calories 60; Total Fat 3g (Saturated Fat 0.5g; Trans Fat 0.5g); Cholesterol 0mg; Sodium 35mg; Total Carbohydrate 7g (Dietary Fiber 0g) **Exchanges:** ½ Other Carbohydrate, ½ Fat **Carbohydrate Choices:** ½

meringue ghosts

Prep Time: 20 Minutes
Start to Finish: 2 Hours 20 Minutes

About 2 dozen cookies

2 egg whites
⅛ teaspoon cream of tartar
½ cup sugar
¼ teaspoon vanilla
**1 teaspoon miniature semisweet
   chocolate chips**

1 Place oven rack in center of oven. Heat oven to 200°F. Line 2 cookie sheets with cooking parchment paper.

2 In small bowl, beat egg whites and cream of tartar with electric mixer on medium speed until foamy. Gradually add sugar, 1 tablespoon at a time, beating on high speed until meringue is very stiff and glossy and sugar is dissolved. On low speed, beat in vanilla just until well mixed.

3 Use disposable decorating bag or gallon-size resealable food-storage plastic bag with ½-inch hole cut in bottom corner. Spoon meringue into bag; twist top to partially close bag. Squeeze bag to pipe meringue into 4-inch ghosts on parchment paper–lined cookie sheets. Place 3 chocolate chips in each ghost for eyes and mouth. Place cookie sheets on center rack in oven.

4 Bake 2 hours. Place parchment paper and cookies on cooling racks. Cool completely, about 10 minutes. Carefully remove cookies from parchment paper. Meringue becomes tough if it absorbs moisture; store in a loosely covered container at room temperature. If the humidity is high, transfer to a tightly covered container.

High Altitude (3500–6500 ft): No change.

■■■ **take note:** Cold eggs are easier to separate but room-temperature egg whites beat to their highest volume. After separating the eggs, let the eggs whites stand at room temperature for about 15 minutes before beating them.

1 Cookie: Calories 20; Total Fat 0g (Saturated Fat 0g; Trans Fat 0g); Cholesterol 0mg; Sodium 0mg; Total Carbohydrate 4g (Dietary Fiber 0g) **Exchanges:** Free **Carbohydrate Choices:** 0

candy corn and peanut-topped brownies

Prep Time: 20 Minutes
Start to Finish: 2 Hours 5 Minutes

36 brownies

BROWNIES

>> 1 box (1 lb 2.3 oz) fudge
  brownie mix
Water, vegetable oil and eggs
  called for on brownie mix box
2 cups miniature marshmallows

TOPPING

½ cup packed brown sugar
½ cup light corn syrup
½ cup creamy peanut butter
2 cups Corn Chex® or Rice Chex®
  cereal
1½ cups salted peanuts
1 cup candy corn

1. Heat oven to 350°F. Spray bottom only of 13×9-inch pan with cooking spray. Make brownie mix as directed on box, using water, oil and eggs. Bake as directed.

2. Remove pan from oven. Immediately sprinkle marshmallows evenly over warm brownies. Bake 1 to 2 minutes longer or until marshmallows just begin to puff. Cool while making topping.

3. In 3-quart saucepan, mix brown sugar and corn syrup until well blended. Cook over medium heat, stirring constantly, until mixture comes to a boil. Remove from heat. Stir in peanut butter until well blended. Add cereal, peanuts and candy corn; mix well.

4. Immediately spoon warm topping over marshmallows; spread to cover. Cool completely, about 1 hour 15 minutes. For brownies, cut into 6 rows by 6 rows.

High Altitude (3500–6500 ft): Make brownie mix following High Altitude directions on box for cakelike brownies.

take note: Candy corn is available in various seasonal color combinations. Use traditional orange, yellow and white candy corn for Halloween. Try brown, orange and white candy corn for Thanksgiving. For Christmas, switch to red, green and white candy corn. Store these kid-friendly bars in an airtight container at room temperature.

1 Brownie: Calories 220; Total Fat 10g (Saturated Fat 1.5g; Trans Fat 0g); Cholesterol 10mg; Sodium 110mg; Total Carbohydrate 29g (Dietary Fiber 1g) **Exchanges:** 1 Starch, 1 Other Carbohydrate, 2 Fat **Carbohydrate Choices:** 2

halloween chocolate pretzels

Prep Time: 1 Hour
Start to Finish: 1 Hour

2 dozen cookies

PRETZELS
¾ **cup sugar**
½ **cup butter or margarine,**
softened
½ **teaspoon almond extract**
1 egg
1¾ **cups all-purpose flour**
¼ **cup unsweetened baking cocoa**

ICING
¾ **cup semisweet chocolate chips**
1½ **teaspoons shortening**
Assorted Halloween candy
sprinkles

1 Heat oven to 325°F. In large bowl, beat sugar and butter with electric mixer on medium speed until well blended. Beat in almond extract and egg until well blended. On low speed, beat in flour and cocoa until well blended.

2 Shape dough into 6-inch-long roll. Cut roll into 6 slices; cut each slice into quarters. For each pretzel, shape 1 dough quarter into 10-inch-long rope. Shape rope into U-shape; cross ends and fold over bottom of U to form pretzel. On ungreased cookie sheets, place pretzels 1 inch apart.

3 Bake 8 to 10 minutes or until set and firm to the touch. Cool 1 minute; remove from cookie sheets to cooling racks. Cool completely, about 10 minutes.

4 In small microwavable bowl, microwave chocolate chips and shortening uncovered on High 30 seconds. Stir; continue microwaving, stirring every 10 seconds, until chocolate is melted and can be stirred smooth. Dip tops of pretzels in chocolate. Sprinkle with candy sprinkles. Refrigerate 10 minutes or until chocolate is set before storing.

High Altitude (3500–6500 ft): No change.

Peppermint Chocolate Pretzels: Substitute ½ teaspoon peppermint extract for the almond extract and ½ cup (about 20) crushed round peppermint candies for the candy sprinkles.

■■■ **take note:** Make pretzel cookies for other holidays too and sprinkle with the holiday colors and decors. Use fall leave decors for Thanksgiving, holly leaves and berry decors for Christmas, tiny red hearts for Valentine's Day and pastel colored sugars for Easter.

1 Cookie: Calories 140; Total Fat 7g (Saturated Fat 4g; Trans Fat 0g); Cholesterol 20mg; Sodium 30mg; Total Carbohydrate 18g (Dietary Fiber 1g) **Exchanges:** ½ Starch, ½ Other Carbohydrate, 1½ Fat **Carbohydrate Choices:** 1

easy halloween cookie pizza

Prep Time: 15 Minutes
Start to Finish: 1 Hour 5 Minutes

About 16 servings

COOKIE PIZZA
>> **1 roll (16.5 oz) refrigerated sugar cookies**
½ cup creamy peanut butter
1 cup candy corn
½ cup raisins

ICING
¼ cup vanilla ready-to-spread frosting (from 1-lb container)

1 Heat oven to 350°F. Line 12-inch pizza pan with foil; spray foil with cooking spray. Cut cookie dough into ¼-inch-thick slices; arrange in bottom of greased foil-lined pan. With floured fingers, press slices to form crust.

2 Bake 15 to 20 minutes or until deep golden brown. Cool completely, about 30 minutes.

3 Using foil lining, lift crust from pan; carefully remove foil from crust. Place crust on serving platter or tray. Spread peanut butter evenly over crust. Sprinkle evenly with candy corn and raisins.

4 In 1-quart saucepan, heat frosting over low heat, stirring constantly, until smooth and thin enough to drizzle. Drizzle icing over cookie pizza. Cut into wedges or squares.

High Altitude (3500–6500 ft): No change.

Christmas Cookie Pizza: Substitute 2 cups white miniature marshmallows for the peanut butter, 1 cup holiday-colored candy-coated chocolate candies for the candy corn and ½ cup dry-roasted peanuts for the raisins. Bake the crust as directed, then immediately sprinkle marshmallows evenly over warm crust; bake 1 to 2 minutes longer or until marshmallows just begin to puff. Cool 5 minutes. Remove crust from pan and place on serving plate. Sprinkle with chocolate candies and peanuts.

Easter Cookie Pizza: Substitute 2 cups pastel-colored miniature marshmallows for the peanut butter, 1 cup spring-colored candy-coated chocolate candies for the candy corn and ½ cup spring-colored miniature jelly beans for the raisins. Bake the crust as directed, then immediately sprinkle marshmallows evenly over warm crust; bake 1 to 2 minutes longer or until marshmallows just begin to puff. Cool 5 minutes. Remove crust from pan and place on serving plate. Sprinkle with chocolate candies and jelly beans.

■■■ **take note:** You can melt the frosting in the microwave. Place frosting in small microwavable bowl; microwave uncovered on High for 10 to 15 seconds or until frosting is thin and can be stirred to drizzling consistency.

1 Serving: Calories 260; Total Fat 11g (Saturated Fat 3g; Trans Fat 1.5g); Cholesterol 10mg; Sodium 135mg; Total Carbohydrate 38g (Dietary Fiber 0g) **Exchanges:** 1 Starch, 1½ Other Carbohydrate, 2 Fat **Carbohydrate Choices:** 2½

shamrock mint cookies

Prep Time: 55 Minutes
Start to Finish: 2 Hours 55 Minutes

About 3 dozen cookies

¾ cup granulated sugar
¾ cup packed brown sugar
1 cup butter or margarine,
   softened
½ teaspoon mint extract
¼ teaspoon green food color
2 eggs
3¾ cups all-purpose flour
1½ teaspoons baking powder
¾ teaspoon salt
3 tablespoons granulated sugar
¼ cup green sugar

1   In large bowl, beat ¾ cup granulated sugar, the brown sugar and butter with electric mixer on medium speed until light and fluffy. Beat in mint extract, food color and eggs until well blended. On low speed, beat in flour, baking powder and salt until well blended. Cover with plastic wrap; refrigerate at least 2 hours for easier handling.

2   Heat oven to 375°F. Shape dough into 1-inch balls. For each cookie, place 3 balls, sides touching, in triangular shape on ungreased cookie sheet. Repeat with remaining dough, placing cookies 2 inches apart. With bottom of glass dipped in sugar, flatten each three-leaved cookie. With sharp knife, score each leaf in half without cutting through. Sprinkle with green sugar.

3   Bake 6 to 10 minutes or until light golden brown. Cool 1 minute; remove from cookie sheets to cooling racks.

High Altitude (3500–6500 ft): No change.

1 Cookie: Calories 140; Total Fat 6g (Saturated Fat 3.5g; Trans Fat 0g); Cholesterol 25mg; Sodium 110mg; Total Carbohydrate 21g (Dietary Fiber 0g) **Exchanges:** ½ Starch, 1 Other Carbohydrate, 1 Fat **Carbohydrate Choices:** 1½

easy frosted irish cream brownies

Prep Time: 15 Minutes
Start to Finish: 2 Hours

48 brownies

BROWNIES
>> 1 box (1 lb 2.3 oz) fudge
   brownie mix
½ cup vegetable oil
¼ cup Irish cream liqueur*
2 eggs

FROSTING
½ cup butter or margarine,
   softened
2 cups powdered sugar
2 tablespoons Irish cream
   liqueur**
½ teaspoon vanilla
2 to 3 teaspoons milk

GLAZE
1 oz semisweet baking chocolate,
   chopped
1 teaspoon butter or margarine

1. Heat oven to 350°F. Spray bottom only of 13×9-inch pan with cooking spray. In large bowl, stir together brownie ingredients; beat 50 strokes with spoon. Spread in pan.

2. Bake 24 to 26 minutes or until brownies are set and begin to pull away from sides of pan (do not overbake). Cool completely, about 45 minutes.

3. In small bowl, beat ½ cup butter with electric mixer on medium speed until light and fluffy. Beat in remaining frosting ingredients, adding enough milk until smooth and spreadable. Spread over brownies.

4. In small microwavable bowl, microwave glaze ingredients uncovered on High 30 seconds; stir until melted and smooth. Drizzle over frosted brownies. Refrigerate 30 minutes or until firm. For bars, cut into 8 rows by 6 rows.

High Altitude (3500–6500 ft): For brownies, add 3 tablespoons all-purpose flour to dry brownie mix. Decrease oil to ¼ cup.

*For ¼ cup Irish cream liqueur, substitute 2 tablespoons Irish cream coffee flavoring syrup and 2 tablespoons half-and-half.

**For 2 tablespoons Irish cream liqueur, substitute 1 tablespoon Irish cream coffee flavoring syrup and 1 tablespoon half-and-half.

■■■ **take note:** Brownies are done when edges look dry and start to pull away from the sides of the pan. Bake the brownies for the minimum time recommended, and then check the edges. Overbaked brownies are dry and hard, so be sure to remove the brownies from the oven as soon as the edges are done.

1 Brownie: Calories 110; Total Fat 5g (Saturated Fat 2g; Trans Fat 0g); Cholesterol 15mg; Sodium 55mg; Total Carbohydrate 15g (Dietary Fiber 0g) **Exchanges:** 1 Other Carbohydrate, 1 Fat **Carbohydrate Choices:** 1

easy chocolate-dipped heart cookies

Prep Time: 1 Hour
Start to Finish: 1 Hour

About 28 cookies

>> **1 roll (16.5 oz) refrigerated sugar cookies**
¼ cup all-purpose flour
Additional ¼ cup all-purpose flour for rolling dough
1½ cups semisweet chocolate chips
1 tablespoon shortening
Candy sprinkles, if desired

1 Heat oven to 350°F. In large bowl, break up cookie dough. Stir or knead in ¼ cup flour until well blended. Remove half the dough; refrigerate remaining dough until needed.

2 Sprinkle 2 tablespoons flour over work surface. Roll half of dough to ⅛-inch thickness, using lightly floured rolling pin. Cut dough with floured 3-inch heart-shaped cookie cutter. Gently brush excess flour from hearts. On ungreased cookie sheets, place hearts 2 inches apart. Repeat with remaining dough and 2 tablespoons flour.

3 Bake 7 to 9 minutes or until light golden brown. Cool 1 minute; remove from cookie sheets to cooling racks. Cool completely, about 15 minutes.

4 Place sheet of waxed paper on cookie sheet. In 1-quart saucepan, heat chocolate chips and shortening over low heat, stirring occasionally, until chips are melted and smooth. Remove from heat. Dip half of each cookie into melted chocolate; allow excess chocolate to drip off. Place on waxed paper. Sprinkle with candy sprinkles. Refrigerate until set.

High Altitude (3500–6500 ft): No change.

Personalized Heart Cookies: Omit the chocolate chips and shortening. Mix ½ cup powdered sugar and 1 to 2 tablespoons milk until smooth and spreadable. Frost cookies; sprinkle red colored sugar around edges of cookies if desired. Let stand until frosting is set. With red decorating gel, write names on the cookies.

■■■ **take note:** Try other flavors of refrigerated cookie dough, such as peanut butter and chocolate chip, to make these easy heart cookies the kids will love.

1 Cookie: Calories 130; Total Fat 7g (Saturated Fat 2.5g; Trans Fat 1g); Cholesterol 5mg; Sodium 55mg; Total Carbohydrate 18g (Dietary Fiber 0g) **Exchanges:** ½ Starch, ½ Other Carbohydrate, 1½ Fat **Carbohydrate Choices:** 1

easy chocolate-almond layered hearts

Prep Time: 1 Hour
Start to Finish: 1 Hour 40 Minutes

About 2½ dozen sandwich cookies

>> **1 roll (16.5 oz) refrigerated sugar cookies**
3 tablespoons all-purpose flour
¼ cup finely chopped almonds
½ teaspoon almond extract
2 tablespoons unsweetened baking cocoa
½ cup semisweet chocolate chips
½ teaspoon vegetable oil

1 Heat oven to 350°F. Remove ⅔ of cookie dough from wrapper and place in medium bowl; refrigerate remaining dough until needed. Into dough in bowl, stir or knead in flour, almonds and almond extract until well blended.

2 On floured surface, roll dough to ¼-inch thickness (about 12-inch round), using lightly floured rolling pin. Cut with floured 2½-inch heart-shaped cookie cutter; place on ungreased cookie sheets.

3 Bake almond hearts 7 to 9 minutes or until edges are light golden brown. Cool 1 minute; remove from cookie sheets to cooling racks.

4 Meanwhile, in small bowl, place remaining ⅓ of dough. Stir or knead in cocoa until well blended. On floured surface, roll dough to ¼-inch thickness (about 8-inch round). Cut with floured 1-inch heart-shaped cookie cutter; place on ungreased large cookie sheet.

5 Bake chocolate hearts 5 to 6 minutes or just until set. Cool 1 minute; remove from cookie sheet to cooling rack.

6 Place chocolate chips and oil in small resealable freezer plastic bag; seal bag. Microwave on High 30 seconds or until chips are softened. Squeeze bag until mixture is smooth. (If necessary, microwave 10 to 15 seconds longer.) Cut ⅛-inch tip from one bottom corner of bag.

7 Squeeze bag to pipe small amount of chocolate on center of each large heart cookie. Top each with 1 small heart cookie. Drizzle remaining melted chocolate over layered cookies. Let stand about 40 minutes or until chocolate is set.

High Altitude (3500–6500 ft): In step 3, bake 8 to 10 minutes.

■■■ **take note:** Any remaining scraps of dough can be rerolled and cut into small hearts. Bake as directed, then assemble into sandwich cookies with leftover melted chocolate or ready-to-spread frosting.

1 Sandwich Cookie: Calories 100; Total Fat 4.5g (Saturated Fat 1.5g; Trans Fat 1g); Cholesterol 5mg; Sodium 50mg; Total Carbohydrate 12g (Dietary Fiber 0g) **Exchanges:** 1 Other Carbohydrate, 1 Fat **Carbohydrate Choices:** 1

(top left) No-Bake After-Dinner Mint Bars, page 152; *(top right)* Pistachio Bars, page 164; *(bottom)* Heavenly Butterscotch Layered Bars, page 156

brownies and bars

fudgy brownies

Prep Time: 30 Minutes
Start to Finish: 2 Hours

24 brownies

BROWNIES
4 oz unsweetened baking
   chocolate
½ cup butter or margarine
2 cups sugar
2 teaspoons vanilla
4 eggs
1 cup all-purpose flour
¼ teaspoon salt

GLAZE
½ cup semisweet chocolate chips
1 tablespoon butter or margarine

1. Heat oven to 350°F. Spray bottom and sides of 13×9-inch pan with cooking spray.

2. In 1-quart saucepan, heat unsweetened chocolate and ½ cup butter over low heat, stirring frequently, until melted and smooth. Remove from heat. Cool slightly, about 10 minutes.

3. In medium bowl, beat sugar, vanilla and eggs with electric mixer on medium speed until light and fluffy. On low speed, beat in flour, salt and chocolate mixture until well blended. Spread in pan.

4. Bake 30 to 38 minutes or just until brownies begin to pull away from sides of pan (do not overbake). Brownies will be barely moist in the center and will continue to firm up as they cool. Cool completely, about 1 hour.

5. In 1-quart saucepan, heat glaze ingredients over low heat, stirring frequently, until melted and smooth. Drizzle glaze over brownies; let stand until set. For brownies, cut into 6 rows by 4 rows.

High Altitude (3500–6500 ft): No change.

■■■ **take note:** Brownies freeze very well. Wrap them individually in plastic wrap, then pop them into a heavy-duty freezer bag. Defrost in the microwave for a quick fix when the next chocolate attack hits.

1 Brownie: Calories 190; Total Fat 9g (Saturated Fat 5g; Trans Fat 0g); Cholesterol 45mg; Sodium 65mg; Total Carbohydrate 24g (Dietary Fiber 1g) **Exchanges:** ½ Starch, 1 Other Carbohydrate, 2 Fat **Carbohydrate Choices:** 1½

double-chocolate and caramel brownies

Prep Time: 30 Minutes
Start to Finish: 3 Hours

24 brownies

FILLING
1 bag (14 oz) caramels,
   unwrapped
½ cup evaporated milk

BROWNIES
1 cup butter or margarine
2 cups sugar
2 teaspoons vanilla
4 eggs, slightly beaten
1¼ cups all-purpose flour
¾ cup unsweetened baking cocoa
¼ teaspoon salt
1 bag (11.5 or 12 oz) semisweet
   chocolate chunks (2 cups)
1½ cups chopped pecans
1 teaspoon vegetable oil

1 Heat oven to 350°F. Spray bottom and sides of 13×9-inch pan with cooking spray. In 1-quart saucepan, heat caramels and milk over low heat, stirring frequently, until caramels are melted and smooth. Remove from heat.

2 In 2-quart saucepan, melt butter over low heat. Remove from heat. Stir in sugar, vanilla and eggs until well blended. Stir in flour, cocoa and salt until well blended. Stir in 1½ cups of the chocolate chunks and 1 cup of the pecans. Spread batter in pan.

3 Gently and evenly drizzle caramel filling over batter to prevent large pockets of caramel and to prevent caramel from reaching bottom of bars. (Caramel can cover entire surface of batter.)

4 Bake 35 to 40 minutes or until set.

5 In 1-quart saucepan, heat remaining ½ cup chocolate chunks and the oil over low heat, stirring frequently, until chocolate is melted and smooth. Drizzle over warm brownies. Sprinkle with remaining ½ cup pecans; press in lightly. Cool 20 minutes.

6 Refrigerate 1 hour 30 minutes or until chocolate is set. For brownies, cut into 6 rows by 4 rows. If refrigerated longer, let stand at room temperature 20 minutes before serving.

High Altitude (3500–6500 ft): Increase flour to 1½ cups.

■■■ **take note:** If the melted caramel mixture has started to set up when you're ready to pour it over the brownie batter, reheat it slightly over low heat.

1 Brownie: Calories 380; Total Fat 20g (Saturated Fat 9g; Trans Fat 0g); Cholesterol 60mg; Sodium 140mg; Total Carbohydrate 46g (Dietary Fiber 2g) **Exchanges:** 1 Starch, 2 Other Carbohydrate, 4 Fat **Carbohydrate Choices:** 3

cappuccino fudge brownies

Prep Time: 40 Minutes
Start to Finish: 2 Hours 30 Minutes

36 brownies

BROWNIES

5 oz unsweetened baking
   chocolate, cut into pieces
¾ cup butter or margarine
2 tablespoons instant coffee
   granules or crystals
1 tablespoon vanilla
2¼ cups granulated sugar
1 teaspoon ground cinnamon
4 eggs
1⅓ cups all-purpose flour
1½ cups coarsely chopped pecans

FROSTING

½ cup butter or margarine,
   softened
2 cups powdered sugar
½ teaspoon vanilla
2 tablespoons cold brewed coffee

GLAZE

1 oz semisweet baking chocolate,
   chopped
1 teaspoon shortening

1 Heat oven to 375°F. Spray bottom and sides of 13×9-inch pan with cooking spray.

2 In 1-quart saucepan, melt unsweetened chocolate and ¾ cup butter over low heat, stirring occasionally. Remove from heat. Stir in coffee granules and 1 tablespoon vanilla; set aside.

3 In large bowl, beat granulated sugar, cinnamon and eggs with electric mixer on medium speed about 7 minutes or until sugar is dissolved. Fold in chocolate mixture, flour and pecans just until blended. Pour batter into pan. Bake 25 to 35 minutes or just until brownies begin to pull away from sides of pan (do not overbake). Cool completely, about 1 hour.

4 In small bowl, beat ½ cup butter with electric mixer on medium speed until light and fluffy. Add powdered sugar, ½ teaspoon vanilla and brewed coffee; beat until smooth. Spread over brownies.

5 In 1-quart saucepan, melt semisweet chocolate and shortening over low heat, stirring occasionally. Drizzle glaze in horizontal parallel lines about 1 inch apart over top of brownies. Immediately draw knife through glaze in straight vertical lines to form pattern. Refrigerate about 15 minutes or until firm. For brownies, cut into 9 rows by 4 rows. Store covered in refrigerator.

High Altitude (3500–6500 ft): No change.

1 Brownie: Calories 230; Total Fat 13g (Saturated Fat 6g; Trans Fat 0g); Cholesterol 40mg; Sodium 55mg; Total Carbohydrate 25g (Dietary Fiber 1g) **Exchanges:** 1 Starch, ½ Other Carbohydrate, 2½ Fat **Carbohydrate Choices:** 1½

triple-layered brownies

Prep Time: 35 Minutes
Start to Finish: 2 Hours 35 Minutes

48 brownies

BROWNIES
½ cup butter or margarine
2 oz unsweetened baking
  chocolate
2 eggs
1 cup packed light brown sugar
½ cup all-purpose flour
1 teaspoon vanilla

FILLING
½ cup whipping cream
1 bag (12 oz) white vanilla baking
  chips (2 cups)
1 cup dried cherries, chopped

GLAZE
½ cup semisweet chocolate chips
2 tablespoons butter or margarine

1 Heat oven to 350°F. Spray bottom and sides of 9-inch square pan with baking spray with flour.

2 In 2-quart saucepan, melt ½ cup butter and the unsweetened chocolate over medium heat, stirring constantly. Remove from heat; cool 5 minutes. Stir in eggs, brown sugar, flour and vanilla until smooth. Spread evenly in pan.

3 Bake 25 to 30 minutes or until toothpick inserted in center comes out clean. Cool in pan on cooling rack about 30 minutes.

4 Meanwhile, in 1-quart saucepan, heat whipping cream and white baking chips just to boiling over medium heat, stirring frequently. Remove from heat. Stir in cherries. Spread filling over brownies. Refrigerate about 30 minutes or until set.

5 In small microwavable bowl, microwave chocolate chips and 2 tablespoons butter uncovered on High 30 seconds; stir. Microwave 15 seconds longer; stir until melted and smooth. Spread glaze evenly over filling. Refrigerate at least 30 minutes. For brownies, cut into 8 rows by 6 rows. Store covered in refrigerator.

High Altitude (3500–6500 ft): No change.

■■■ **take note:** You can substitute 1 cup cherry-flavored or unflavored dried sweetened cranberries, chopped, for the cherries, if you like.

1 Brownie: Calories 120; Total Fat 6g (Saturated Fat 4g; Trans Fat 0g); Cholesterol 20mg; Sodium 40mg; Total Carbohydrate 13g (Dietary Fiber 0g) **Exchanges:** ½ Starch, ½ Other Carbohydrate, 1 Fat **Carbohydrate Choices:** 1

cheesecake brownies

Prep Time: 20 Minutes
Start to Finish: 6 Hours

24 brownies

TOPPING
1 package (8 oz) cream cheese, softened
2 tablespoons butter or margarine, softened
½ cup sugar
1 teaspoon vanilla
2 eggs

BROWNIES
4 oz semisweet baking chocolate
3 tablespoons butter or margarine
½ cup sugar
1 teaspoon vanilla
2 eggs
½ cup all-purpose flour
½ teaspoon baking powder
¼ teaspoon salt

GLAZE
1 oz semisweet baking chocolate
2 teaspoons butter or margarine

1 Heat oven to 350°F. Spray bottom and sides of 9-inch square pan with baking spray with flour. In small bowl, mix topping ingredients until well blended; set aside.

2 In 2-quart saucepan, heat 4 oz chocolate and 3 tablespoons butter over low heat, stirring frequently, until melted and smooth. Remove from heat; cool 15 minutes. Stir in ½ cup sugar and the vanilla until well blended. Beat in 2 eggs, one at a time, blending well after each addition. Stir in flour, baking powder and salt just until blended. Pour into pan. Pour topping over batter.

3 Bake 40 to 50 minutes or until toothpick inserted in center comes out clean. Cool completely, about 1 hour.

4 In 1-quart saucepan, heat glaze ingredients over low heat, stirring frequently, until melted and smooth. Drizzle glaze over brownies. Refrigerate at least 4 hours. For brownies, cut into 6 rows by 4 rows. Store covered in refrigerator.

High Altitude (3500–6500 ft): Increase flour to ½ cup plus 2 tablespoons.

Apricot Cheesecake Brownies: Substitute ½ cup apricot preserves for the glaze. Remove brownies from the oven. Stir the preserves and spread evenly over the hot brownies. Refrigerate at least 3 hours.

Espresso Cheesecake Brownies: Add ½ teaspoon instant espresso coffee granules with the sugar in the topping and ½ teaspoon espresso granules with the sugar in the brownies.

1 Brownie: Calories 150; Total Fat 9g (Saturated Fat 5g; Trans Fat 0g); Cholesterol 55mg; Sodium 95mg; Total Carbohydrate 14g (Dietary Fiber 0g) **Exchanges:** 1 Other Carbohydrate, 2 Fat **Carbohydrate Choices:** 1

chocolate brownies with peanut butter filling

Prep Time: 35 Minutes
Start to Finish: 2 Hours 50 Minutes

36 brownies

BROWNIES
½ cup dark corn syrup
½ cup butter or margarine
6 oz bittersweet baking
   chocolate, coarsely chopped
3 eggs
1 cup all-purpose flour
¾ cup granulated sugar
1 teaspoon vanilla

FILLING
2 cups chunky peanut butter
½ cup butter or margarine,
   softened
2 cups powdered sugar
1 tablespoon vanilla

FROSTING
½ cup whipping cream
6 oz bittersweet baking
   chocolate, coarsely chopped
1 teaspoon vanilla
Chopped roasted peanuts,
   if desired

1 Heat oven to 325°F. Spray bottom and sides of 13×9-inch pan with baking spray with flour.

2 In 2-quart saucepan, heat corn syrup, ½ cup butter and 6 oz chocolate over low heat, stirring frequently, until chocolate is melted. Remove from heat. Beat in eggs, one at a time, with wire whisk. Add flour, granulated sugar and 1 teaspoon vanilla; beat with wire whisk until batter is smooth and shiny. Spread in pan.

3 Bake 23 to 25 minutes or just until toothpick inserted in center comes out clean (do not overbake). Cool completely, about 45 minutes.

4 Meanwhile, in large bowl, beat peanut butter and ½ cup butter with electric mixer on medium speed until blended. Add powdered sugar and 1 tablespoon vanilla; beat until smooth and fluffy. Spread over brownies.

5 In 1-quart saucepan, heat whipping cream and 6 oz chocolate over low heat, stirring frequently, until chocolate is melted and mixture is smooth. Stir in 1 teaspoon vanilla. Cool 5 minutes. Spread frosting over filling. Sprinkle with peanuts. Refrigerate about 1 hour or until firm. For brownies, cut into 6 rows by 6 rows, using a thin-bladed knife dipped into warm water.

High Altitude (3500–6500 ft): Heat oven to 350°F. Bake 27 to 29 minutes.

■■■ **take note:** When measuring corn syrup, coat your measuring cup with cooking spray and the syrup will pour out of the cup easily.

1 Brownie: Calories 290; Total Fat 19g (Saturated Fat 9g; Trans Fat 0g); Cholesterol 35mg; Sodium 115mg; Total Carbohydrate 23g (Dietary Fiber 2g) **Exchanges:** ½ Starch, 1 Other Carbohydrate, ½ High-Fat Meat, 3 Fat **Carbohydrate Choices:** 1½

white chocolate–cherry blondies

Prep Time: 30 Minutes
Start to Finish: 4 Hours 55 Minutes

36 blondies

2 cups packed brown sugar
**½ cup butter or margarine,
  softened**
2 teaspoons vanilla
½ teaspoon almond extract
2 eggs
2 cups all-purpose flour
1 teaspoon baking powder
¼ teaspoon salt
**2 packages (6 oz each) white
  chocolate baking bars,
  cut into chunks**
½ cup slivered almonds
½ cup chopped dried cherries
½ teaspoon vegetable oil

1 Heat oven to 350°F. Spray bottom and sides of 13×9-inch pan with cooking spray.

2 In large bowl, beat brown sugar, butter, vanilla, almond extract and eggs with electric mixer on medium speed until light and fluffy. On low speed, beat in flour, baking powder and salt until well blended. Set aside ¼ cup of white chocolate chunks. Stir remaining chunks, almonds and cherries into batter. Spread batter evenly in pan.

3 Bake 20 to 25 minutes or until top is golden brown and set. Cool completely, about 1 hour.

4 In small microwavable bowl, microwave reserved white chocolate chunks and oil uncovered on High 30 to 60 seconds, stirring every 15 seconds, until melted; stir well. Drizzle glaze over bars. (Or if desired, place glaze in small food-storage plastic bag and cut off small tip from one corner of bag; drizzle glaze in diagonal lines over bars.) Let stand about 3 hours or until glaze is set. For bars, cut into 6 rows by 6 rows.

High Altitude (3500–6500 ft): Spread batter in pan to within ½ inch of edges (batter will spread during baking). Bake 30 to 35 minutes.

White Chocolate–Blueberry Blondies: Substitute ½ cup chopped dried blueberries for the cherries.

White Chocolate–Cranberry Blondies: Substitute ½ cup chopped sweetened dried cranberries for the cherries.

■■■ **take note:** The slivered almonds can be whole or chopped, or left out completely if you like.

1 Blondie: Calories 170; Total Fat 7g (Saturated Fat 3.5g; Trans Fat 0g); Cholesterol 20mg; Sodium 65mg; Total Carbohydrate 25g (Dietary Fiber 0g) **Exchanges:** ½ Starch, 1 Other Carbohydrate, 1½ Fat **Carbohydrate Choices:** 1½

sunburst lemon bars

Prep Time: 15 Minutes
Start to Finish: 2 Hours

36 bars

CRUST
2 cups all-purpose flour
1 cup butter or margarine,
    softened
½ cup powdered sugar

FILLING
4 eggs
2 cups granulated sugar
¼ cup all-purpose flour
1 teaspoon baking powder
¼ cup lemon juice

GLAZE
1 cup powdered sugar
2 to 3 tablespoons lemon juice

1 Heat oven to 350°F. In large bowl, beat crust ingredients with electric mixer on low speed until crumbly. Press mixture evenly in bottom of ungreased 13×9-inch pan. Bake 20 to 30 minutes or until light golden brown.

2 Meanwhile, in large bowl, lightly beat eggs with wire whisk. Beat in remaining filling ingredients except lemon juice until well blended. Beat in ¼ cup lemon juice.

3 Remove partially baked crust from oven. Pour filling evenly over warm crust.

4 Bake 25 to 30 minutes longer or until top is light golden brown. Cool completely, about 1 hour.

5 In small bowl, mix 1 cup powdered sugar and enough lemon juice until glaze is smooth and spreadable. Spread glaze over bars. For bars, cut into 6 rows by 6 rows.

High Altitude (3500–6500 ft): No change.

take note: It's best to use fresh lemon juice for these bars. One medium lemon yields 2 to 3 tablespoons of juice, so you'll need 2 large or 3 medium lemons. For a more intense lemony flavor, add finely shredded lemon peel to the filling.

1 Bar: Calories 150; Total Fat 6g (Saturated Fat 3.5g; Trans Fat 0g); Cholesterol 35mg; Sodium 55mg; Total Carbohydrate 22g (Dietary Fiber 0g) **Exchanges:** ½ Starch, 1 Other Carbohydrate, 1 Fat **Carbohydrate Choices:** 1½

margarita olé bars

Prep Time: 15 Minutes
Start to Finish: 2 Hours

36 bars

CRUST
1¾ cups all-purpose flour
½ cup powdered sugar
1 cup butter or margarine,
   softened

FILLING
4 eggs
1½ cups granulated sugar
¼ cup all-purpose flour
½ teaspoon baking powder
⅓ cup frozen margarita mix
   concentrate, thawed
2 teaspoons grated lime peel
1 tablespoon powdered sugar

1 Heat oven to 350°F. In large bowl, mix crust ingredients with electric mixer on low speed until crumbly. With floured fingers, press mixture firmly in bottom of ungreased 13×9-inch pan. Bake 20 to 25 minutes or until light golden brown.

2 Meanwhile, in large bowl, beat eggs slightly. Mix in granulated sugar, ¼ cup flour and the baking powder until well blended. Stir in margarita mix and lime peel.

3 Remove partially baked crust from oven. Pour filling over warm crust.

4 Bake 18 to 22 minutes longer or until top is golden brown and filling is set. Cool completely, about 1 hour. Just before serving, sprinkle with 1 tablespoon powdered sugar. For bars, cut into 6 rows by 6 rows.

High Altitude (3500–6500 ft): No change.

■■■ **take note:** Spoon out ⅓ cup of the margarita mix to thaw for the recipe. Transfer the remaining margarita mix to a small freezer container for later use. You can use ⅓ cup frozen limeade concentrate, thawed, if you don't have margarita mix.

1 Bar: Calories 130; Total Fat 6g (Saturated Fat 3.5g; Trans Fat 0g); Cholesterol 35mg; Sodium 50mg; Total Carbohydrate 17g (Dietary Fiber 0g) **Exchanges:** 1 Other Carbohydrate, ½ Fat **Carbohydrate Choices:** 1

strawberry-almond crumble bars

Prep Time: 30 Minutes
Start to Finish: 2 Hours 35 Minutes

24 bars

FILLING
¾ cup strawberry preserves
2 cups frozen whole unsweetened
   strawberries, slightly thawed,
   finely chopped
4 teaspoons cornstarch

CRUST AND TOPPING
1 cup slivered almonds
2 cups all-purpose flour
1 cup powdered sugar
½ teaspoon baking powder
1 cup cold butter or margarine,
   cut into 1-inch pieces, slightly
   softened

1   Heat oven to 350°F. Line 13×9-inch pan with 18×18-inch piece of heavy-duty foil so foil extends over long sides of pan. Spray foil with cooking spray.

2   If preserves contain large strawberry pieces, break them apart with a spoon for more even coverage. In 1-quart saucepan, mix strawberries, preserves and cornstarch. Heat to boiling over medium heat, stirring frequently. Cook 1 to 2 minutes, stirring constantly, until slightly thickened. Set aside to cool.

3   Meanwhile, place almonds on ungreased cookie sheet. Bake 6 to 9 minutes, stirring occasionally, until light brown. Cool completely, about 10 minutes.

4   In food processor, process ¾ cup of the almonds 5 to 10 seconds or until finely chopped. Add flour, powdered sugar and baking powder; process 10 seconds or until well mixed. Add butter; process with on-and-off pulses until mixture is crumbly. Reserve 2 cups of the mixture for topping. Press remaining mixture in pan. Spread strawberry mixture over crust. Crumble reserved flour mixture over filling. Sprinkle with remaining almonds; press gently.

5   Bake 32 to 40 minutes or until light golden brown. Cool completely, about 1 hour 15 minutes. Lift foil with bars from pan. For bars, cut into 6 rows by 4 rows. Store covered in refrigerator.

High Altitude (3500–6500 ft): After pressing crust mixture in pan, bake 10 minutes before adding filling.

■■■ **take note:** Soften the butter just enough so when you pinch it with your fingers, it will have a little "give." It shouldn't be so soft that you could spread it. This will provide the best texture for the crust and topping.

1 Bar: Calories 190; Total Fat 10g (Saturated Fat 5g; Trans Fat 0g); Cholesterol 20mg; Sodium 70mg; Total Carbohydrate 23g (Dietary Fiber 1g) **Exchanges:** ½ Starch, 1 Other Carbohydrate, 2 Fat **Carbohydrate Choices:** 1½

caramel apple bars

Prep Time: 30 Minutes
Start to Finish: 1 Hour 55 Minutes

48 bars

CRUST AND TOPPING
2 cups all-purpose flour
2 cups quick-cooking oats
1½ cups packed brown sugar
1¼ cups butter or margarine, melted
1 teaspoon baking soda

FILLING
1½ cups caramel topping
½ cup all-purpose flour
2 cups coarsely chopped peeled cooking apples (2 medium)
½ cup chopped walnuts or pecans

1 Heat oven to 350°F. Spray bottom and sides of 15×10×1-inch pan with cooking spray.

2 In large bowl, beat crust and topping ingredients with electric mixer on low speed, scraping bowl occasionally, until crumbly. Press half of mixture (about 2½ cups) evenly in bottom of pan; reserve remaining mixture for topping. Bake 8 minutes.

3 Meanwhile, in 1-quart saucepan, mix caramel topping and ½ cup flour until well blended. Heat to boiling over medium heat, stirring constantly. Boil 3 to 5 minutes, stirring constantly, until mixture thickens slightly.

4 Remove partially baked crust from oven. Sprinkle apples and walnuts over warm crust; pour caramel mixture evenly over top. Sprinkle with reserved topping mixture.

5 Bake 20 to 25 minutes longer or until golden brown. Cool 30 minutes. Refrigerate about 30 minutes or until set. For bars, cut into 8 rows by 6 rows.

High Altitude (3500–6500 ft): Heat oven to 375°F.

■■■ **take note:** Use tart, firm-textured apples to complement the sweetness of the caramel. Granny Smith, Braeburn, Cortland and Haralson are good choices.

1 Bar: Calories 150; Total Fat 6g (Saturated Fat 3g; Trans Fat 0g); Cholesterol 15mg; Sodium 100mg; Total Carbohydrate 22g (Dietary Fiber 0g) **Exchanges:** ½ Starch, 1 Other Carbohydrate, 1 Fat **Carbohydrate Choices:** 1½

spicy pumpkin bars

Prep Time: 30 Minutes
Start to Finish: 2 Hours 30 Minutes

48 bars

BARS
2 cups all-purpose flour
1½ cups packed brown sugar
½ cup apple juice
½ cup vegetable oil
2 teaspoons baking powder
2 teaspoons pumpkin pie spice
1 teaspoon baking soda
¼ teaspoon salt
2 eggs
1 can (15 oz) pumpkin (not
  pumpkin pie mix)

FROSTING
1 package (3 oz) cream cheese,
  softened
2 tablespoons butter or
  margarine, softened
½ teaspoon vanilla
3 cups powdered sugar
1 to 2 tablespoons milk
Ground nutmeg, if desired

1 Heat oven to 350°F. Spray bottom and sides of 15×10×1-inch pan with baking spray with flour.

2 In large bowl, beat bar ingredients with electric mixer on low speed until moistened. Beat on medium speed 2 minutes. Spread batter in pan.

3 Bake 20 to 30 minutes or until toothpick inserted in center comes out clean. Cool completely, about 1 hour.

4 In medium bowl, mix cream cheese and butter until blended. Stir in vanilla. Gradually beat in powdered sugar and enough milk until frosting is smooth and spreadable. Spread frosting over bars. Sprinkle with nutmeg. Refrigerate about 30 minutes or until set. For bars, cut into 8 rows by 6 rows. Store covered in refrigerator.

High Altitude (3500–6500 ft): Increase flour to 2⅓ cups. Decrease baking powder to 1 teaspoon.

▪▪▪ **take note:** If you don't have pumpkin pie spice, use 1 teaspoon ground cinnamon, ½ teaspoon ground nutmeg and ½ teaspoon ground cloves instead. And to save time, use 1 container (1 pound) cream cheese creamy ready-to-spread frosting for the scratch frosting.

1 Bar: Calories 120; Total Fat 3.5g (Saturated Fat 1g; Trans Fat 0g); Cholesterol 10mg; Sodium 75mg; Total Carbohydrate 19g (Dietary Fiber 0g) **Exchanges:** ½ Starch, 1 Other Carbohydrate, ½ Fat **Carbohydrate Choices:** 1

rocky road s'more bars

Prep Time: 20 Minutes
Start to Finish: 1 Hour 40 Minutes

32 bars

BARS
1½ cups all-purpose flour
⅔ cup packed brown sugar
½ teaspoon baking powder
½ teaspoon salt
¼ teaspoon baking soda
½ cup butter or margarine, softened
1 teaspoon vanilla
2 egg yolks
3 cups miniature marshmallows
1 cup milk chocolate chips

TOPPING
⅔ cup light corn syrup
¼ cup butter or margarine
2 teaspoons vanilla
1 bag (11.5 oz) milk chocolate chips (2 cups)
2 cups Golden Grahams® cereal
1 cup salted peanuts

1 Heat oven to 350°F. In large bowl, beat all bar ingredients except marshmallows and chocolate chips with electric mixer on low speed until crumbly. Press mixture firmly in bottom of ungreased 13×9-inch pan. Bake 12 to 15 minutes or until light golden brown.

2 Remove partially baked bars from oven. Immediately sprinkle with marshmallows and 1 cup chocolate chips.

3 Bake 1 to 2 minutes longer or until marshmallows just begin to puff. Remove from oven; cool while preparing topping.

4 In 3-quart saucepan, cook all topping ingredients except cereal and peanuts over medium heat 2 to 3 minutes, stirring constantly, until butter and chocolate chips are melted. Stir in cereal and peanuts. Immediately spoon warm topping evenly over bars; spread gently to cover. Refrigerate about 1 hour or until firm. For bars, cut into 8 rows by 4 rows.

High Altitude (3500–6500 ft): No change.

1 Bar: Calories 240; Total Fat 12g (Saturated Fat 5g; Trans Fat 0g); Cholesterol 30mg; Sodium 140mg; Total Carbohydrate 30g (Dietary Fiber 1g) **Exchanges:** 1 Starch, 1 Other Carbohydrate, 2 Fat **Carbohydrate Choices:** 2

peanut butter and jelly bars

Prep Time: 10 Minutes
Start to Finish: 1 Hour

24 bars

>> 1 roll (16.5 oz) refrigerated
    peanut butter cookies
½ cup peanut butter chips
¼ cup creamy peanut butter
1 container (1 lb) vanilla creamy
    ready-to-spread frosting
¼ cup strawberry jelly or seedless
    raspberry jam

1   Heat oven to 350°F (325°F for dark pan). Spray bottom and sides of 13×9-inch pan with cooking spray.

2   Break up cookie dough in pan; press evenly in pan. Press peanut butter chips evenly into dough. Bake 15 to 20 minutes or until golden brown. Cool completely, about 30 minutes.

3   In medium bowl, stir peanut butter until smooth. Stir in frosting until well blended. Spread over cooled bars.

4   In small bowl, stir jelly until smooth. Drop jelly by teaspoonfuls over frosting. With tip of knife, swirl jelly for a marbled design. For bars, cut into 6 rows by 4 rows.

High Altitude (3500–6500 ft): Stir 2 tablespoons all-purpose flour into cookie dough before pressing in pan.

Chocolate, Peanut Butter and Jelly Bars: Substitute ½ cup semisweet chocolate chips for the peanut butter chips and 1 container (1 lb) chocolate creamy ready-to-spread frosting for the vanilla frosting.

■■■ **take note:** Everyone has a favorite flavor jelly or jam so use any flavor you like for these family-favorite bars.

1 Bar: Calories 230; Total Fat 11g (Saturated Fat 4.5g; Trans Fat 0.5g); Cholesterol 0mg; Sodium 125mg; Total Carbohydrate 29g (Dietary Fiber 0g) **Exchanges:** 1 Starch, 1 Other Carbohydrate, 2 Fat **Carbohydrate Choices:** 2

candy-topped peanut butter bars

Prep Time: 30 Minutes
Start to Finish: 2 Hours 20 Minutes

36 bars

>> **1 roll (16.5 oz) refrigerated
   chocolate chip cookies**
**¾ cup butter or margarine,
   softened**
½ cup peanut butter
2 cups powdered sugar
2 tablespoons milk
1 cup salted peanuts
1 cup semisweet chocolate chips
¼ cup whipping cream
**½ cup miniature candy-coated
   chocolate baking bits**

1 Heat oven to 350°F. In ungreased 13×9-inch pan, break up cookie dough. With floured fingers, press dough evenly in bottom of pan to form crust. Bake 12 to 16 minutes or until light golden brown. Cool completely, about 30 minutes.

2 In medium bowl, beat ½ cup of the butter, the peanut butter, powdered sugar and milk until smooth. Stir in peanuts. Spread mixture over cooled crust.

3 In 1-quart saucepan, heat chocolate chips and remaining ¼ cup butter over low heat, stirring frequently, until melted and smooth. Remove from heat. Cool 10 minutes.

4 Stir whipping cream into chocolate mixture until well blended. Spread over peanut butter mixture. Immediately sprinkle baking bits over chocolate. Refrigerate about 1 hour or until chocolate is set. For bars, cut into 6 rows by 6 rows. Store covered in refrigerator.

High Altitude (3500–6500 ft): Bake crust 16 to 19 minutes.

Peanut-Topped Peanut Butter Bars: Substitute ½ cup crunchy peanut butter for the peanut butter and salted peanuts in the filling. Omit the candy-coated chocolate baking bits, and sprinkle the 1 cup salted peanuts on top of the chocolate mixture.

1 Bar: Calories 210; Total Fat 13g (Saturated Fat 6g; Trans Fat 1g); Cholesterol 15mg; Sodium 100mg; Total Carbohydrate 21g (Dietary Fiber 1g) **Exchanges:** ½ Starch, 1 Other Carbohydrate, 2½ Fat **Carbohydrate Choices:** 1½

peanut brittle bars

Prep Time: 10 Minutes
Start to Finish: 1 Hour 45 Minutes

48 bars

CRUST
2 cups all-purpose flour
1 cup packed brown sugar
1 teaspoon baking soda
¼ teaspoon salt
1 cup butter or margarine

TOPPING
2 cups salted peanuts
1 cup milk chocolate chips
1 jar (12.25 oz) caramel topping
3 tablespoons all-purpose flour

1 Heat oven to 350°F. Spray bottom and sides of 15×10×1-inch pan with cooking spray.

2 In large bowl, mix all crust ingredients except butter. Cut in butter, using pastry blender or fork, until crumbly. Press mixture evenly in bottom of pan. Bake 8 to 14 minutes or until golden brown.

3 Remove partially baked crust from oven. Sprinkle peanuts and chocolate chips over crust to within ¼ inch of sides of pan. In small bowl, mix caramel topping and 3 tablespoons flour until well blended. Drizzle evenly over chocolate chips and peanuts.

4 Bake 12 to 18 minutes longer or until topping is set and golden brown. Cool completely, about 1 hour. For bars, cut into 8 rows by 6 rows.

High Altitude (3500–6500 ft): No change.

Cashew Brittle Bars: Substitute 2 cups salted cashews for the peanuts and 1 cup semisweet chocolate chips for the milk chocolate chips.

1 Bar: Calories 150; Total Fat 8g (Saturated Fat 3.5g; Trans Fat 0g); Cholesterol 10mg; Sodium 115mg; Total Carbohydrate 17g (Dietary Fiber 1g) **Exchanges:** 1 Starch, 1½ Fat **Carbohydrate Choices:** 1

Extra Special Brownies

Prepare and bake (1 pound 6.5 ounce) supreme brownie mix with pouch of chocolate flavor syrup as directed on box. Make it extra special with one of the following toppings.

Cherry Brownies: Beat 1½ cups whipping cream until stiff. Gently stir in 1½ cups miniature marshmallows and ½ cup well-drained chopped maraschino cherries. Spread on cooled brownies; drizzle with chocolate topping.

Butterscotch Brownies: Heat ⅔ cup sugar and ⅔ cup light corn syrup to boiling, stirring constantly; remove from heat. Stir in 1 cup butterscotch chips and ½ cup peanut butter until melted; gently stir in 2 cups corn flakes cereal. Immediately spread over cooled brownies.

Rocky Road Brownies: Remove from oven and immediately sprinkle with 2 cups miniature marshmallows, 1 cup semisweet chocolate chips and 1½ cups chopped peanuts. Cool completely.

Raspberry-Cream Cheese Brownies: Beat an 8-ounce package cream cheese, softened, ½ cup powdered sugar and ½ cup raspberry preserves; spread over cooled brownies. Refrigerate 15 minutes. Melt 1 cup semisweet chocolate chips and 1 teaspoon shortening until smooth; drizzle over brownies.

no-bake after-dinner mint bars

Prep Time: 30 Minutes
Start to Finish: 45 Minutes

25 bars

½ cup butter or margarine
1 bag (10 oz) mint-flavored
   semisweet chocolate chips
   (1⅔ cups)
2 cups thin chocolate wafer
   cookie crumbs (about
   32 cookies)
¼ cup butter or margarine,
   softened
1 tablespoon milk
½ teaspoon peppermint extract
½ teaspoon vanilla
1 drop green food color
2 cups powdered sugar
⅓ cup butter or margarine

1 Lightly spray bottom and sides of 9-inch square pan with cooking spray. In 2-quart saucepan, melt ½ cup butter and ¼ cup of the chocolate chips over low heat, stirring constantly. Remove from heat. Stir in cookie crumbs until well mixed; press evenly in pan. Refrigerate about 10 minutes or until firm.

2 Meanwhile, in small bowl, beat ¼ cup butter, the milk, peppermint extract, vanilla and food color with electric mixer on medium speed until well mixed. On low speed, gradually beat in powdered sugar until smooth. Spread peppermint mixture evenly over crumb mixture.

3 In 1-quart saucepan, melt remaining chocolate chips and ⅓ cup butter over low heat, stirring constantly; spread evenly over peppermint mixture. Refrigerate 10 to 15 minutes or until chocolate is set. For bars, cut into 5 rows by 5 rows.

High Altitude (3500–6500 ft): No change.

take note: You can melt the chocolate chips and butter for the both the cookie crumb base and frosting in a microwavable bowl. Microwave on High 1 minute. Stir; microwave an additional 10 to 20 seconds, stirring after each additional time, until melted and smooth.

1 Bar: Calories 210; Total Fat 13g (Saturated Fat 7g; Trans Fat 0g); Cholesterol 25mg; Sodium 125mg; Total Carbohydrate 23g (Dietary Fiber 1g) **Exchanges:** ½ Other Carbohydrate, 2½ Fat **Carbohydrate Choices:** 1½

chocolate cheesecake bars

Prep Time: 30 Minutes
Start to Finish: 3 Hours 20 Minutes

24 bars

CRUST
2 cups thin chocolate wafer cookie crumbs (about 32 cookies)
¼ cup granulated sugar
½ cup butter or margarine, melted

FILLING
3 packages (8 oz each) cream cheese, softened
1 can (14 oz) sweetened condensed milk (not evaporated)
2 oz unsweetened baking chocolate, melted, slightly cooled
2 teaspoons vanilla
3 eggs

TOPPING
2 oz unsweetened baking chocolate
2 tablespoons butter or margarine
3 tablespoons water
1¾ cups powdered sugar

1 Heat oven to 300°F. In ungreased 13×9-inch pan, mix crust ingredients. Press firmly in bottom of pan.

2 In large bowl, beat cream cheese with electric mixer on medium speed until fluffy. Add milk, melted chocolate, vanilla and eggs; beat until smooth, scraping side of bowl frequently. Pour filling over crust.

3 Bake 40 to 50 minutes or until set. Cool 30 minutes.

4 In 1-quart saucepan, heat 2 oz chocolate and 2 tablespoons butter over low heat, stirring frequently, until melted and smooth. Remove from heat. Add water and powdered sugar; beat until smooth.

5 Spread topping over warm cheesecake. Refrigerate 1 hour 30 minutes or until chilled. Let stand at room temperature 15 minutes before cutting and serving so the fudge topping adheres to the cheesecake. For bars, cut into 6 rows by 4 rows. Store covered in refrigerator.

High Altitude (3500–6500 ft): Bake 45 to 55 minutes.

1 Bar: Calories 320; Total Fat 20g (Saturated Fat 12g; Trans Fat 0.5g); Cholesterol 75mg; Sodium 210mg; Total Carbohydrate 29g (Dietary Fiber 1g) **Exchanges:** ½ Starch, 1½ Other Carbohydrate, ½ High-Fat Meat, 3 Fat **Carbohydrate Choices:** 2

maple-walnut pie bars

Prep Time: 10 Minutes
Start to Finish: 2 Hours 25 Minutes

36 bars

>>
1 roll (16.5 oz) refrigerated sugar
    cookies
3 eggs
⅓ cup packed brown sugar
2 tablespoons all-purpose flour
1⅓ cups maple-flavored syrup
1½ cups chopped walnuts
Powdered sugar, if desired

1 Heat oven to 350°F. In ungreased 13×9-inch pan, break up cookie dough. With floured fingers, press dough evenly in bottom of pan. Bake 13 to 15 minutes or until edges are golden brown.

2 Meanwhile, in large bowl, beat eggs with wire whisk. Stir in brown sugar, flour and syrup until well blended. Stir in walnuts.

3 Remove partially baked crust from oven. Pour egg mixture evenly over crust.

4 Bake 30 to 35 minutes longer or until filling is set. Cool completely on cooling rack, about 1 hour 30 minutes. Sprinkle with powdered sugar. For bars, cut into 6 rows by 6 rows.

High Altitude (3500–6500 ft): No change.

Maple-Peanut Pie Bars: Substitute 1½ cups salted peanuts for the walnuts.

Maple-Pecan Pie Bars: Substitute 1½ cups chopped pecans for the walnuts.

■■■ **take note:** A small wire strainer works great for sprinkling the powdered sugar evenly over the bars.

1 Bar: Calories 140; Total Fat 6g (Saturated Fat 1g; Trans Fat 0.5g); Cholesterol 20mg; Sodium 55mg; Total Carbohydrate 20g (Dietary Fiber 0g) **Exchanges:** ½ Starch, 1 Other Carbohydrate, 1 Fat **Carbohydrate Choices:** 1

heavenly butterscotch layered bars

Prep Time: 10 Minutes
Start to Finish: 2 Hours 50 Minutes

36 bars

>>
1 roll (16.5 oz) refrigerated
  chocolate chip cookies
½ cup thin chocolate wafer cookie
  crumbs (about 8 cookies)
1 bag (11 oz) butterscotch chips
  (2 cups)
1½ cups flaked coconut
½ cup chopped walnuts
1 can (14 oz) sweetened condensed
  milk (not evaporated)

1 Heat oven to 350°F. Line bottom and sides of 13×9-inch pan with heavy-duty foil, extending foil over sides of pan. Spray bottom and sides of foil with cooking spray.

2 In pan, break up cookie dough. With floured fingers, press dough evenly in bottom of pan to form crust. Sprinkle cookie crumbs evenly over crust. Top evenly with butterscotch chips, coconut and walnuts. Drizzle milk over top.

3 Bake 30 to 40 minutes or until edges are golden brown (center will not be set). Cool completely, about 2 hours. Use foil to lift bars from pan. For bars, cut into 6 rows by 6 rows.

High Altitude (3500–6500 ft): No change.

Heavenly Chocolate Layered Bars: Substitute 1 bag (12 oz) semisweet chocolate chips for the butterscotch chips.

■■■ **take note:** Package these favorite bars in a pretty box, and take to the next bake sale.

1 Bar: Calories 180; Total Fat 9g (Saturated Fat 5g; Trans Fat 0.5g); Cholesterol 5mg; Sodium 80mg; Total Carbohydrate 22g (Dietary Fiber 0g) **Exchanges:** ½ Starch, 1 Other Carbohydrate, 2 Fat **Carbohydrate Choices:** 1½

chocolaty caramel-pecan bars

Prep Time: 30 Minutes
Start to Finish: 1 Hour 30 Minutes

24 bars

CRUST
½ cup powdered sugar
½ cup butter or margarine,
   softened
1 tablespoon whipping cream
1 cup all-purpose flour

FILLING
24 caramels, unwrapped
⅓ cup whipping cream
2 cups pecan halves

TOPPING
1 teaspoon butter or margarine
½ cup milk chocolate chips
2 tablespoons whipping cream

1 Bar: Calories 200; Total Fat 13g (Saturated Fat 5g; Trans Fat 0g); Cholesterol 20mg; Sodium 60mg; Total Carbohydrate 18g (Dietary Fiber 1g) **Exchanges:** 1 Starch, 2½ Fat **Carbohydrate Choices:** 1

1 Heat oven to 325°F. Spray bottom and sides of 9-inch square pan with cooking spray.

2 In medium bowl, mix powdered sugar, ½ cup butter and 1 tablespoon whipping cream until well blended. Add flour; mix until crumbly. With floured hands, press mixture evenly in pan. Bake 15 to 20 minutes or until firm to the touch.

3 Meanwhile, in 2-quart saucepan, heat caramels and ⅓ cup whipping cream over low heat, stirring frequently, until caramels are melted and mixture is smooth. Remove from heat. Add pecans; stir well to coat. Immediately spoon over baked crust; spread carefully to cover.

4 In 1-quart saucepan, melt 1 teaspoon butter and the chocolate chips over low heat, stirring constantly. Stir in 2 tablespoons whipping cream. Drizzle topping over filling. Refrigerate about 1 hour or until filling is firm. For bars, cut into 6 rows by 4 rows.

High Altitude (3500–6500 ft): No change.

more brownies and bars

dulce de leche bars

Prep Time: 20 Minutes
Start to Finish: 1 Hour 35 Minutes

32 bars

1½ cups all-purpose flour
1½ cups quick-cooking or
    old-fashioned oats
1 cup packed brown sugar
¼ teaspoon salt
1 cup butter or margarine,
    softened
1 can (13.4 oz) dulce de leche
    (caramelized sweetened
    condensed milk)
1 cup toffee bits

1 Heat oven to 350°F. In large bowl, mix flour, oats, brown sugar and salt. Cut in butter, using pastry blender or fork, until mixture is crumbly. In ungreased 13×9-inch pan, press ¾ of mixture. Bake 10 minutes. (Reserve remaining crumb mixture for topping.)

2 Meanwhile, in 1-quart saucepan, heat dulce de leche over low heat 2 to 4 minutes, stirring frequently, until slightly softened.

3 Remove partially baked crust from oven. Spread dulce de leche over crust. Sprinkle evenly with toffee bits and remaining crumb mixture. Bake 20 to 25 minutes longer or until golden brown. Cool 15 minutes.

4 Run knife around sides of pan to loosen bars. Cool completely, about 30 minutes. For bars, cut into 8 rows by 4 rows.

High Altitude (3500–6500 ft): Decrease butter to ½ cup. In step 2, heat dulce de leche over medium-low heat 4 to 6 minutes.

■ ■ ■ **take note:** Dulce de leche is caramelized sweetened condensed milk and can be found in the baking section of the grocery store near the condensed milk. If it isn't available, use 1 jar (12 ounces) dulce de leche–flavored ice cream topping.

1 Bar: Calories 190; Total Fat 9g (Saturated Fat 5g; Trans Fat 0g); Cholesterol 20mg; Sodium 105mg; Total Carbohydrate 24g (Dietary Fiber 0g) **Exchanges:** ½ Starch, 1 Other Carbohydrate, 2 Fat **Carbohydrate Choices:** 1½

pecan-rum bars

Prep Time: 40 Minutes
Start to Finish: 2 Hours 15 Minutes

32 bars

CRUST
1 cup butter or margarine,
   softened
1 cup packed brown sugar
2 cups all-purpose flour

FILLING
2 eggs
½ cup packed brown sugar
½ cup dark corn syrup
1 tablespoon rum or 1 teaspoon
   rum extract
2 cups pecan halves

ICING
½ cup powdered sugar
1 tablespoon butter or margarine,
   softened
2 teaspoons rum or ½ teaspoon
   rum extract plus 2 teaspoons
   water

1 Heat oven to 375°F. Spray bottom and sides of 13×9-inch pan with cooking spray (do not use dark pan).

2 In medium bowl, beat 1 cup butter and 1 cup brown sugar with electric mixer on low speed until creamy. Stir in flour. Press evenly in pan. Bake 12 to 14 minutes or until edges are golden brown and center springs back when touched lightly.

3 Meanwhile, in medium bowl, mix all filling ingredients except pecans. Stir in pecans.

4 Remove partially baked crust from oven. Pour filling over crust, spreading pecans evenly.

5 Bake 12 to 15 minutes longer or until filling is set. Cool completely, about 1 hour.

6 In small bowl, mix icing ingredients (add additional rum or water, ½ teaspoon at a time, if icing is too thick to drizzle). Drizzle icing over bars. For bars, cut into 8 rows by 4 rows.

High Altitude (3500–6500 ft): No change.

■■■ **take note:** These bars freeze well; wrap tightly, label and freeze up to 6 months. Thaw at room temperature when you are ready to serve them.

1 Bar: Calories 200; Total Fat 11g (Saturated Fat 4.5g; Trans Fat 0g); Cholesterol 30mg; Sodium 55mg; Total Carbohydrate 23g (Dietary Fiber 0g) **Exchanges:** ½ Starch, 1 Other Carbohydrate, 2 Fat **Carbohydrate Choices:** 1½

white chocolate–cashew-pretzel bars

Prep Time: 25 Minutes
Start to Finish: 1 Hour 40 Minutes

36 bars

>> 1 roll (16.5 oz) refrigerated sugar
   cookies
1 bag (12 oz) vanilla baking chips
1 cup coarsely chopped pretzel
   sticks or twists
1½ cups semisweet chocolate
   chips
¼ cup peanut butter
1 cup chopped cashews

1 Heat oven to 350°F. Spray bottom and sides of 13×9-inch pan with cooking spray.

2 Break up cookie dough in pan. With floured fingers, press dough evenly in bottom of pan to form crust. Sprinkle 1 cup of the vanilla baking chips and the pretzels over dough; lightly press into dough. Bake 16 to 20 minutes or until light golden brown. Cool completely on wire rack, about 30 minutes.

3 In small microwavable bowl, place ¼ cup of the vanilla baking chips; set aside. In large microwavable bowl, microwave remaining vanilla baking chips and the chocolate chips uncovered on High 2 minutes, stirring every 30 seconds, until melted and smooth. If necessary, microwave 30 seconds longer. Stir in peanut butter and cashews. Spread mixture evenly over cooled baked crust. Refrigerate about 15 minutes or until chocolate is set.

4 Microwave reserved ¼ cup vanilla baking chips uncovered on High 30 seconds; stir until melted and smooth. If necessary, microwave 10 seconds longer. Drizzle over bars. Let stand about 10 minutes or until set. For bars, cut into 6 rows by 6 rows.

High Altitude (3500–6500 ft): No change.

White Chocolate–Peanut-Pretzel Bars: Substitute 1 roll (16.5 oz) refrigerated peanut butter cookies for the sugar cookies and 1 cup dry-roasted peanuts for the cashews.

1 Bar: Calories 190; Total Fat 10g (Saturated Fat 4g; Trans Fat 0.5g); Cholesterol 5mg; Sodium 85mg; Total Carbohydrate 21g (Dietary Fiber 0g) **Exchanges:** ½ Starch, 1 Other Carbohydrate, 2 Fat **Carbohydrate Choices:** 1½

chocolate toffee bars

Prep Time: 20 Minutes
Start to Finish: 1 Hour 35 Minutes

36 bars

CRUST
1 cup all-purpose flour
½ cup packed brown sugar
½ cup butter or margarine,
  softened

TOPPING
1 cup packed brown sugar
2 tablespoons all-purpose flour
1 teaspoon baking powder
2 eggs
1 cup semisweet chocolate
  chips (6 oz)
½ cup chopped nuts

1 Heat oven to 350°F. In small bowl, mix crust ingredients until well blended. Press in bottom of ungreased 13×9-inch pan. Bake 8 to 10 minutes or until lightly browned. Cool slightly, about 5 minutes. Increase oven temperature to 375°F.

2 Meanwhile, in medium bowl, mix 1 cup brown sugar, 2 tablespoons flour, the baking powder and eggs until well blended. Stir in chocolate chips and nuts. Pour topping evenly over crust, spreading slightly if necessary.

3 Bake 13 to 18 minutes or until deep golden brown and center is set. Cool completely, about 1 hour. For bars, cut into 6 rows by 6 rows.

High Altitude (3500–6500 ft): In crust, decrease butter to ⅓ cup. In topping, increase flour to 3 tablespoons.

■■■ **take note:** Place 1 to 3 cups of brown sugar in microwavable bowl. Cover with damp paper towel, then plastic wrap. Microwave on High 1 minute. Let stand 2 minutes until softened. Repeat once or twice if necessary.

1 Bar: Calories 110; Total Fat 5g (Saturated Fat 2.5g; Trans Fat 0g); Cholesterol 20mg; Sodium 40mg; Total Carbohydrate 15g (Dietary Fiber 0g) **Exchanges:** ½ Starch, ½ Other Carbohydrate, 1 Fat **Carbohydrate Choices:** 1

pistachio bars

Prep Time: 25 Minutes
Start to Finish: 2 Hours 20 Minutes

25 bars

CRUST
1 cup all-purpose flour
¼ cup sugar
½ cup butter or margarine

TOPPING
1 egg
¼ cup sugar
¼ cup corn syrup
1 tablespoon butter or margarine, melted
¼ teaspoon vanilla
1 cup coarsely chopped pistachio nuts
½ cup flaked coconut

1 Heat oven to 350°F. In medium bowl, mix flour and ¼ cup sugar. Cut in ½ cup butter, using pastry blender or fork, until mixture looks like coarse crumbs. Press mixture in bottom of ungreased 8-inch square pan.

2 Bake 20 to 25 minutes or until light golden brown. Cool 10 minutes.

3 Meanwhile, in medium bowl, beat egg slightly. Stir in remaining topping ingredients except nuts and coconut until well blended. Stir in nuts and coconut.

4 Remove partially baked crust from oven. Spoon and spread coconut mixture evenly over warm crust.

5 Bake 15 to 20 minutes longer or until edges are golden brown. Cool completely, about 1 hour 15 minutes. For bars, cut into 5 rows by 5 rows.

High Altitude (3500–6500 ft): No change.

■■■ **take note:** During winter holidays, use red-dyed pistachios, natural green pistachios or a combination of both for a festive bar. Store pistachios sealed in an airtight container in a cool spot, or freeze them for longer storage.

1 Bar: Calories 120; Total Fat 7g (Saturated Fat 3.5g; Trans Fat 0g); Cholesterol 20mg; Sodium 40mg; Total Carbohydrate 13g (Dietary Fiber 0g) **Exchanges:** 1 Other Carbohydrate, 1½ Fat **Carbohydrate Choices:** 1

brickle bars

Prep Time: 10 Minutes
Start to Finish: 1 Hour 20 Minutes

36 bars

BARS
½ cup granulated sugar
½ cup packed brown sugar
½ cup butter or margarine,
    softened
2 teaspoons vanilla
2 eggs
1½ cups all-purpose flour
2 teaspoons baking powder
¼ teaspoon salt
½ cup toffee bits

TOPPING
¾ cup semisweet chocolate chips
⅓ cup toffee bits

1 Heat oven to 350°F. Spray bottom and sides of 13×9-inch pan with cooking spray.

2 In large bowl, beat granulated sugar, brown sugar and butter with electric mixer on medium speed until well blended. Beat in vanilla and eggs until light and fluffy. On low speed, beat in flour, baking powder and salt until dough forms. Stir in ½ cup toffee bits. Spread in pan.

3 Bake 20 to 25 minutes or until golden brown and toothpick inserted in center comes out clean.

4 Remove pan from oven. Immediately sprinkle with chocolate chips; let stand 1 minute. Spread melted chips over bars. Sprinkle ⅓ cup toffee bits evenly over top. Cool completely, about 45 minutes. For bars, cut into 6 rows by 6 rows.

High Altitude (3500–6500 ft): Decrease granulated sugar and brown sugar to ⅓ cup each.

Pecan Bars: Substitute ½ cup chopped pecans for the toffee bits in the bars. Sprinkle ¼ cup chopped pecans on top with the chocolate chips and toffee bits.

■■■ **take note:** Do a "taste test" before adding toffee bits to your recipe because they can become rancid. Store toffee bits in the freezer to prevent this. Store bars in a single layer in an airtight container.

1 Bar: Calories 120; Total Fat 6g (Saturated Fat 3.5g; Trans Fat 0g); Cholesterol 20mg; Sodium 90mg; Total Carbohydrate 15g (Dietary Fiber 0g) **Exchanges:** ½ Starch, ½ Other Carbohydrate, 1 Fat **Carbohydrate Choices:** 1

(top left) Frosted Ginger Cookies, page 200; *(top right)* Black and White Chunk Cookies, page 170; *(bottom)* Maple-Walnut Shortbread Cookies, page 184 ❯

any occasion cookies

candy bar–oatmeal cookies

Prep Time: 50 Minutes
Start to Finish: 50 Minutes

About 3 dozen cookies

1 cup packed brown sugar
½ cup granulated sugar
¾ cup butter or margarine,
   softened
1 tablespoon milk
1 teaspoon vanilla
2 eggs
2¼ cups all-purpose flour
1 teaspoon baking soda
2 cups old-fashioned or
   quick-cooking oats
1 bag (11.2 oz) fun-size milk
   chocolate-covered peanut,
   caramel and nougat candy
   bars, unwrapped, each cut
   into 8 pieces

1 Heat oven to 350°F. Spray cookie sheets with cooking spray.

2 In large bowl, beat brown sugar, granulated sugar and butter with electric mixer on medium speed until light and fluffy. Beat in milk, vanilla and eggs until well blended. On low speed, beat in flour and baking soda until well blended. Stir in oats. Stir in candy pieces.

3 On cookie sheets, drop dough by heaping tablespoonfuls 2 inches apart.

4 Bake 10 to 12 minutes or until light golden brown. Cool 2 minutes; remove from cookie sheets to cooling racks.

High Altitude (3500–6500 ft): Flatten cookies to about ½-inch thickness before baking.

■■■ **take note:** If you want to use the larger snack-size candy bars instead of the fun-size bars, cut them into ½-inch cubes. Feel free to experiment with your favorite candy bar.

1 Cookie: Calories 160; Total Fat 7g (Saturated Fat 3.5g; Trans Fat 0g); Cholesterol 20mg; Sodium 85mg; Total Carbohydrate 23g (Dietary Fiber 1g) **Exchanges:** ½ Starch, 1 Other Carbohydrate, 1½ Fat **Carbohydrate Choices:** 1½

cashew–white chocolate drops

Prep Time: 50 Minutes
Start to Finish: 50 Minutes

About 3 dozen cookies

¾ cup packed brown sugar
½ cup granulated sugar
1 cup butter or margarine,
   softened
2 teaspoons milk
1 teaspoon vanilla
1 egg
2 cups all-purpose flour
1 teaspoon baking soda
1 cup coarsely chopped cashew
   halves and pieces
6 oz white chocolate baking bars,
   coarsely chopped (1 cup)

1 Heat oven to 375°F. In large bowl, beat brown sugar, granulated sugar and butter with electric mixer on medium speed until light and fluffy. Beat in milk, vanilla and egg until well blended. On low speed, beat in flour and baking soda until well blended. Stir in cashews and white chocolate.

2 On ungreased cookie sheets, drop dough by rounded tablespoonfuls 2 inches apart.

3 Bake 8 to 10 minutes or until light golden brown. Cool 1 minute; remove from cookie sheets to cooling racks.

High Altitude (3500–6500 ft): Decrease butter to ¾ cup.

Pecan-Chocolate Drops: Substitute 1 cup coarsely chopped pecans for the cashews and 1 cup semisweet chocolate chunks for the white chocolate.

1 Cookie: Calories 150; Total Fat 9g (Saturated Fat 4.5g; Trans Fat 0g); Cholesterol 20mg; Sodium 80mg; Total Carbohydrate 16g (Dietary Fiber 0g) **Exchanges:** 1 Starch, 1½ Fat **Carbohydrate Choices:** 1

black and white chunk cookies

Prep Time: 55 Minutes
Start to Finish: 55 Minutes

About 3 dozen cookies

¾ cup packed brown sugar
½ cup granulated sugar
½ cup butter or margarine,
  softened
½ cup shortening
1½ teaspoons vanilla
1 egg
1¾ cups all-purpose flour
1 teaspoon baking soda
¼ teaspoon salt
4 oz semisweet baking chocolate,
  chopped
4 oz white chocolate baking bars,
  chopped
1 cup chopped pecans

1 Heat oven to 375°F. In large bowl, beat brown sugar, granulated sugar, butter and shortening with electric mixer on medium speed until light and fluffy. Beat in vanilla and egg until well blended. On low speed, beat in flour, baking soda and salt until well blended. Stir in semisweet chocolate, white chocolate and pecans.

2 On ungreased cookie sheets, drop dough by rounded tablespoonfuls 2 inches apart.

3 Bake 9 to 12 minutes or until light golden brown. Cool 1 minute; remove from cookie sheets to cooling racks.

High Altitude (3500–6500 ft): Increase flour to 2 cups.

Walnut–Chocolate Chunk Cookies: Omit white chocolate baking bars. Increase semisweet chocolate to 8 oz. Substitute 1 cup chopped walnuts for the pecans.

1 Cookie: Calories 160; Total Fat 10g (Saturated Fat 3.5g; Trans Fat 0.5g); Cholesterol 15mg; Sodium 75mg; Total Carbohydrate 16g (Dietary Fiber 0g) **Exchanges:** ½ Starch, ½ Other Carbohydrate, 2 Fat **Carbohydrate Choices:** 1

chewy coconut–macadamia nut cookies

Prep Time: 1 Hour
Start to Finish: 1 Hour

About 3½ dozen cookies

1 cup butter or margarine,
  softened
¾ cup granulated sugar
¾ cup packed brown sugar
1 teaspoon vanilla
2 eggs
2¼ cups all-purpose flour
1 teaspoon baking soda
1 teaspoon ground cinnamon
½ teaspoon salt
1 cup old-fashioned or quick-
  cooking oats
½ cup coconut
½ cup coarsely chopped
  macadamia nuts

1 Heat oven to 375°F. In large bowl, beat butter, granulated sugar and brown sugar with electric mixer on medium speed until light and fluffy. Beat in vanilla and eggs until well blended. On low speed, beat in flour, baking soda, cinnamon and salt until well blended. Stir in oats, coconut and nuts.

2 On ungreased cookie sheets, drop dough by rounded teaspoonfuls 2 inches apart.

3 Bake 8 to 10 minutes or until golden brown. Cool 2 minutes; remove from cookie sheets to cooling racks.

High Altitude (3500–6500 ft): Increase flour to 2½ cups.

■■■ **take note:** These cookies freeze well and thaw quickly—perfect for surprise guests. Seal the cookies in an airtight container, and freeze them for up to 2 weeks. Let the cookies stand at room temperature for 30 minutes before serving.

1 Cookie: Calories 120; Total Fat 6g (Saturated Fat 3.5g; Trans Fat 0g); Cholesterol 20mg; Sodium 95mg; Total Carbohydrate 15g (Dietary Fiber 0g) **Exchanges:** ½ Starch, ½ Other Carbohydrate, 1 Fat **Carbohydrate Choices:** 1

coconut–chocolate chunk cookies

Prep Time: 1 Hour 5 Minutes
Start to Finish: 1 Hour 35 Minutes

About 2 dozen cookies

COOKIE
¾ **cup packed brown sugar**
½ **cup granulated sugar**
1 **cup butter or margarine,**
   softened
2 **eggs**
2 **cups all-purpose flour**
¼ **cup unsweetened baking cocoa**
1 **teaspoon baking soda**
½ **teaspoon salt**
5 **oz semisweet baking chocolate,**
   chopped
1 **cup honey-roasted peanuts,**
   coarsely chopped
2 **cups coconut**

GLAZE
1 **cup powdered sugar**
1 **to 2 tablespoons water**

1 Heat oven to 350°F. In large bowl, beat brown sugar, granulated sugar and butter with electric mixer on medium speed until light and fluffy. Beat in eggs until well blended. On low speed, beat in flour, cocoa, baking soda and salt until well blended. Stir in chocolate, peanuts and coconut.

2 On ungreased cookie sheets, drop dough by ¼ cupfuls 3 inches apart.

3 Bake 13 to 15 minutes or until set. Cool 1 minute; remove from cookie sheets to cooling racks. Cool completely, about 30 minutes.

4 In small bowl, mix glaze ingredients, adding water 1 tablespoon at a time, until smooth and thin enough to drizzle. Drizzle glaze over cookies.

High Altitude (3500–6500 ft): Decrease baking soda to ¾ teaspoon.

■■■ **take note:** You may want to purchase a #16 spring-handled ice cream scoop to use for dropping dough on cookie sheets. Cookies will be uniform in size, and you'll cut the time needed to get a sheet of dough ready for the oven in half.

1 Cookie: Calories 290; Total Fat 16g (Saturated Fat 9g; Trans Fat 0g); Cholesterol 40mg; Sodium 210mg; Total Carbohydrate 33g (Dietary Fiber 2g) **Exchanges:** 1½ Starch, ½ Other Carbohydrate, 3 Fat **Carbohydrate Choices:** 2

crunchy fudge cookies

Prep Time: 55 Minutes
Start to Finish: 1 Hour 25 Minutes

About 3½ dozen cookies

>> 1 box (1 lb 2.3 oz) fudge
    brownie mix
2 cups Fiber One® cereal
2 tablespoons miniature
    semisweet chocolate chips
⅛ teaspoon ground cinnamon
⅓ cup water
1 tablespoon canola or
    vegetable oil
2 teaspoons vanilla
1 egg

1 Heat oven to 350°F. Spray cookie sheets with cooking spray.

2 In large bowl, mix ingredients with spoon. On cookie sheets, drop dough by rounded tablespoonfuls 2 inches apart.

3 Bake 10 to 12 minutes or until set. Cool 2 minutes; remove from cookie sheets to cooling racks. Cool completely, about 30 minutes.

High Altitude (3500–6500 ft): No change.

■■■ **take note:** No one will guess that the crunchy bits in these fudgy cookies are fiber cereal. Starting with a brownie mix makes these delicious cookies quick and easy.

1 Cookie: Calories 70; Total Fat 1g (Saturated Fat 0g; Trans Fat 0g); Cholesterol 5mg; Sodium 55mg; Total Carbohydrate 13g (Dietary Fiber 2g) **Exchanges:** 1 Other Carbohydrate **Carbohydrate Choices:** 1

cashew cookies with browned butter icing

Prep Time: 40 Minutes
Start to Finish: 40 Minutes

About 2½ dozen cookies

COOKIES
1 roll (16.5 oz) refrigerated sugar cookies
¾ cup coarsely chopped cashews
½ cup chopped white chocolate baking bars or white vanilla baking chips

ICING
⅓ cup butter (do not use margarine)
1½ cups powdered sugar
¼ teaspoon vanilla
2 tablespoons milk

1 Heat oven to 350°F. In large bowl, break up cookie dough. Stir in cashews and white chocolate.

2 On ungreased cookie sheets, drop dough by heaping teaspoonfuls, about 2 inches apart.

3 Bake 9 to 12 minutes or until golden brown. Immediately remove from cookie sheets to cooling racks.

4 Meanwhile, in 1-quart saucepan, heat butter over medium heat, stirring constantly, until light golden brown. Remove from heat. Stir in remaining icing ingredients until smooth.

5 On top of warm cookies, immediately spoon about 1 teaspoon icing (if icing becomes too thick, reheat over low heat).

High Altitude (3500–6500 ft): Bake 10 to 13 minutes.

Walnut Cookies with Browned Butter Icing: Substitute ¾ cup coarsely chopped walnuts for the cashews.

■■■ **take note:** In this recipe, butter is necessary to obtain the browned butter flavor in the icing. Margarine will not provide the same flavor or color and will take longer to brown. Nothing beats the flavor of browned butter icing, but if you need to save time, use a container of butter cream ready-to-spread frosting instead.

1 Cookie: Calories 160; Total Fat 8g (Saturated Fat 3g; Trans Fat 1g); Cholesterol 10mg; Sodium 70mg; Total Carbohydrate 19g (Dietary Fiber 0g) **Exchanges:** ½ Starch, 1 Other Carbohydrate, 1½ Fat **Carbohydrate Choices:** 1

tropical oatmeal cookies

Prep Time: 55 Minutes
Start to Finish: 55 Minutes

About 4 dozen cookies

¾ **cup granulated sugar**
¾ **cup packed brown sugar**
¾ **cup butter or margarine,**
   softened
1 **teaspoon vanilla**
2 **eggs**
2¼ **cups all-purpose flour**
1 **teaspoon baking soda**
2 **cups old-fashioned or**
   quick-cooking oats
1 **cup coconut**
1 **jar (3.25 oz) macadamia nuts,**
   coarsely chopped (about
   ⅔ **cup)**
1 **bag (7 oz) diced dried tropical**
   fruits

1 Heat oven to 375°F. Spray cookie sheets with cooking spray.

2 In large bowl, beat granulated sugar, brown sugar and butter with electric mixer on medium speed until light and fluffy. Beat in vanilla and eggs until well blended. On low speed, beat in flour and baking soda until well blended. Stir in oats, coconut, nuts and dried fruits.

3 On cookie sheets, drop dough by rounded tablespoonfuls 2 inches apart.

4 Bake 7 to 10 minutes or until light golden brown. Cool 1 minute; remove from cookie sheets to cooling racks.

High Altitude (3500–6500 ft): No change.

■■■ **take note:** Diced dried fruit mixtures are convenient for recipes. The packaged mixture used in this recipe contains golden raisins, pineapple, papaya, apricots and mango. And if you like, you can use ⅔ cup chopped walnuts or pecans instead of the macadamia nuts.

1 Cookie: Calories 120; Total Fat 5g (Saturated Fat 2.5g; Trans Fat 0g); Cholesterol 15mg; Sodium 55mg; Total Carbohydrate 17g (Dietary Fiber 1g) **Exchanges:** ½ Starch, ½ Other Carbohydrate, 1 Fat **Carbohydrate Choices:** 1

peanut butter–raisin bran cookies

Prep Time: 55 Minutes
Start to Finish: 55 Hours

About 3 dozen cookies

½ **cup butter or margarine,
  softened**
½ **cup peanut butter**
½ **cup granulated sugar**
½ **cup packed brown sugar**
1 **egg**
¾ **cup all-purpose flour**
¾ **teaspoon baking soda**
½ **teaspoon baking powder**
4 **cups Total® Raisin Bran cereal**

1 Heat oven to 350°F. In large bowl, stir butter, peanut butter, granulated sugar, brown sugar and egg until blended. Stir in flour, baking soda and baking powder. Stir in cereal.

2 On ungreased cookie sheets, drop dough by rounded tablespoonfuls, about 2 inches apart.

3 Bake 11 to 13 minutes or until lightly browned. Cool 2 minutes; remove from cookie sheets to cooling racks.

High Altitude (3500–6500 ft): No change.

■■■ **take note:** You can use either creamy or chunky peanut butter in this chewy cookie. Did you know that you get ¼ serving of whole grain in just one cookie?

1 Cookie: Calories 100; Total Fat 4.5g (Saturated Fat 2g; Trans Fat 0g); Cholesterol 15mg; Sodium 95mg; Total Carbohydrate 12g (Dietary Fiber 0g) **Exchanges:** 1 Other Carbohydrate, 1 Fat **Carbohydrate Choices:** 1

walnut-topped ginger drops

Prep Time: 1 Hour
Start to Finish: 1 Hour

About 3½ dozen cookies

½ **cup packed brown sugar**
½ **cup butter or margarine,**
   softened
1 **teaspoon vanilla**
1 **egg**
2 **cups all-purpose flour**
¼ **cup half-and-half**
3 **tablespoons finely chopped**
   candied ginger
½ **teaspoon baking soda**
½ **teaspoon salt**
½ **teaspoon ground cardamom**
42 **walnut halves**
3 **tablespoons white vanilla**
   baking chips

1　Heat oven to 375°F. In large bowl, beat brown sugar and butter with electric mixer on medium speed until light and fluffy. Beat in vanilla and egg until well blended. On low speed, beat in remaining ingredients except walnuts and baking chips until well blended.

2　On ungreased cookie sheets, drop dough by rounded teaspoonfuls 2 inches apart. Press 1 walnut half onto each cookie.

3　Bake 6 to 9 minutes or until edges are set and light golden brown. Immediately remove from cookie sheets to cooling racks. Cool completely, about 5 minutes.

4　Meanwhile, place baking chips in small resealable freezer plastic bag; seal bag. Microwave on High 30 to 45 seconds or until softened. Squeeze bag until mixture is smooth. (If necessary, microwave 30 seconds longer or just until all chips are melted.) Cut small tip from one bottom corner of bag. Squeeze bag to drizzle melted chips over cookies.

High Altitude (3500–6500 ft): Increase flour to 2 cups plus 2 tablespoons.

■■■ **take note:** Candied ginger is gingerroot that has been cooked in sugar syrup, dried and then coated in sugar. Look for candied ginger near the dried fruit in the produce department of the supermarket.

1 Cookie: Calories 80; Total Fat 4g (Saturated Fat 2g; Trans Fat 0g); Cholesterol 10mg; Sodium 65mg; Total Carbohydrate 8g (Dietary Fiber 0g) **Exchanges:** ½ Starch, 1 Fat **Carbohydrate Choices:** ½

whole wheat zucchini cookies

Prep Time: 1 Hour
Start to Finish: 1 Hour 15 Minutes

About 5 dozen cookies

¾ cup granulated sugar
¾ cup packed brown sugar
1 cup butter or margarine,
    softened
1 teaspoon grated lemon peel
1 teaspoon vanilla
2 eggs
2½ cups whole wheat flour
1 teaspoon baking soda
1 teaspoon ground cinnamon
½ teaspoon salt
2 cups old-fashioned or
    quick-cooking oats
2 cups shredded zucchini (about
    2 medium), drained
1 bag (12 oz) miniature chocolate
    chips (2 cups)

1 Heat oven to 350°F. Lightly spray cookie sheets with cooking spray.

2 In large bowl, beat granulated sugar, brown sugar and butter with electric mixer on medium speed until light and fluffy. Beat in lemon peel, vanilla and eggs until well blended. On low speed, beat in flour, baking soda, cinnamon and salt until well blended. Stir in oats, zucchini and chocolate chips.

3 On cookie sheets, drop dough by rounded teaspoonfuls, about 2 inches apart.

4 Bake 9 to 13 minutes or until golden brown. Immediately remove from cookie sheets to cooling racks. Cool completely, about 15 minutes.

High Altitude (3500–6500 ft): No change.

■ ■ ■ **take note:** Zucchini contains a lot of moisture. To avoid making the batter watery, drain the shredded squash by pressing it down in a colander or sieve set in the sink or over a bowl before mixing it with other ingredients.

1 Cookie: Calories 110; Total Fat 5g (Saturated Fat 3g; Trans Fat 0g); Cholesterol 15mg; Sodium 65mg; Total Carbohydrate 14g (Dietary Fiber 1g) **Exchanges:** ½ Starch, ½ Other Carbohydrate, 1 Fat **Carbohydrate Choices:** 1

cardamom print sandwich cookies

Prep Time: 1 Hour 10 Minutes
Start to Finish: 2 Hour 25 Minutes

About 2 dozen sandwich cookies

COOKIES
1 cup packed brown sugar
1 cup butter or margarine, softened
1 egg
2 cups all-purpose flour
1 teaspoon ground cardamom
1 teaspoon ground cinnamon
¼ cup granulated sugar

FILLING
2 tablespoons butter or margarine
1¼ cups powdered sugar
½ teaspoon vanilla
4 to 5 teaspoons milk

1 In large bowl, beat brown sugar and 1 cup butter with electric mixer on medium speed until light and fluffy. Beat in egg until well blended. On low speed, beat in flour, cardamom and cinnamon until well blended. If necessary, cover with plastic wrap and refrigerate 1 hour for easier handling.

2 Heat oven to 350°F. Shape dough into 1-inch balls; roll in granulated sugar. On ungreased cookie sheets, place balls 2 inches apart. For each cookie, dip bottom of glass that has textured base in granulated sugar; flatten dough ball to form 1½-inch round.

3 Bake 6 to 10 minutes or until firm to the touch. Immediately remove from cookie sheets to cooling racks. Cool completely, about 15 minutes.

4 In 2-quart saucepan, heat 2 tablespoons butter over medium heat, stirring frequently, until light golden brown. Remove from heat. Stir in remaining filling ingredients, adding enough milk until filling is spreadable. For each sandwich cookie, spread about 1 teaspoon filling between 2 cookies.

High Altitude (3500–6500 ft): Bake 8 to 12 minutes.

■■■ **take note:** Use decorative cookie stamps, found at cookware stores, instead of the bottom of a glass to make fun cookie designs. Or flatten the dough balls with a kitchen tool, such as a fork, meat mallet, vegetable crimper or potato masher.

1 Sandwich Cookie: Calories 190; Total Fat 9g (Saturated Fat 6g; Trans Fat 0g); Cholesterol 30mg; Sodium 70mg; Total Carbohydrate 25g (Dietary Fiber 0g) **Exchanges:** ½ Starch, 1 Other Carbohydrate, 2 Fat **Carbohydrate Choices:** 1½

Giving Cookies

Give a gift of homemade cookies in a container that the receiver will enjoy using after the cookies are long gone. You may want to wrap pairs of cookies back-to-back in plastic wrap before tucking them into the container.

Flowerpot: For the gardener, fill a pretty pot with cookies and add a couple packets of seeds around the inside edge of the pot.

Vase: Fill a pretty vase (with a wide opening) with cookies. Tuck a few fresh flowers with stems sealed in water tubes among the cookies.

Tackle Box: Fill a small plastic tackle box with cookies. Tuck in a few colorful fishing flies and a bobber or two.

Toolbox: Fill a small plastic toolbox with cookies. Tuck in some packets of small nails or screws.

Scrapbook Kit: Fill a plastic organizer box with cookies. Tuck in a few appropriate stickers or fun decorative-edge scissors.

Sewing Kit: Fill a plastic organizer box with cookies. Tuck sewing items, such as needles, buttons and thread, among the cookies.

Drawer Organizer: Fill the sections of a divided drawer organizer with cookies. Or fill all but one section with cookies and fill the remaining sections with desk supplies, such as paper clips, rubber bands, pushpins and small notepads.

maple-walnut shortbread cookies

Prep Time: 2 Hours 40 Minutes
Start to Finish: 4 Hours 45 Minutes

4 dozen cookies

1 cup butter or margarine,
  softened
⅓ cup sugar
1½ cups finely chopped toasted
  walnuts
1 egg yolk
2 cups all-purpose flour
1 teaspoon baking powder
¼ teaspoon salt
1 teaspoon maple flavor
1 cup semisweet chocolate
  chips (6 oz)

1 In large bowl, beat butter and sugar with electric mixer on medium speed about 30 seconds or until smooth. Beat in ½ cup of the walnuts and the egg yolk until blended. On low speed, beat in flour, baking powder, salt and maple flavor until stiff cookie dough forms. Shape dough into a ball. Wrap in plastic wrap; refrigerate 45 minutes.

2 Heat oven to 350°F. Divide dough into 8 equal parts. On lightly floured surface, shape each part into a rope 12 inches long and ¾ inch thick. Cut each rope into 2-inch pieces. On ungreased cookie sheets, place dough pieces about 2 inches apart; flatten slightly.

3 Bake 15 to 17 minutes or until edges begin to brown. Cool 2 minutes; remove from cookie sheets to cooling racks. Cool completely, about 30 minutes.

4 Meanwhile, in small microwavable bowl, microwave chocolate chips uncovered on High about 1 minute 30 seconds, stirring every 30 seconds, until chips can be stirred smooth. In another small bowl, place remaining 1 cup walnuts.

5 For each cookie, dip ½ inch of 1 long side into chocolate, then coat chocolate edge with walnuts. Place on sheets of waxed paper; let stand about 2 hours until chocolate is set.

High Altitude (3500–6500 ft): No change.

■■■ **take note:** To toast walnuts, spread in ungreased shallow pan; bake at 350°F for 5 to 8 minutes, stirring occasionally, until aromatic. Finely chop when cooled. Or sprinkle the nuts in an ungreased heavy skillet; cook over medium heat 5 to 7 minutes, stirring frequently, until aromatic.

1 Cookie: Calories 100; Total Fat 7g (Saturated Fat 3.5g; Trans Fat 0g); Cholesterol 15mg; Sodium 50mg; Total Carbohydrate 8g (Dietary Fiber 0g) **Exchanges:** ½ Starch, 1½ Fat **Carbohydrate Choices:** ½

chocolate ganache meringues

Prep Time: 35 Minutes
Start to Finish: 1 Hour 50 Minutes

12 sandwich cookies

GANACHE
¼ **cup whipping cream**
3 **oz bittersweet baking chocolate, cut into pieces**
2 **tablespoons cold butter or margarine, cut into small pieces**

MERINGUES
2 **egg whites**
⅓ **cup granulated sugar**
⅓ **cup powdered sugar**
¼ **cup powdered sugar**
2 **tablespoons unsweetened baking cocoa**

1 In 1-quart heavy saucepan, heat whipping cream over medium heat just until cream comes to a simmer. Remove from heat; stir in chocolate until melted. Stir in butter pieces, a few at a time, until melted. Refrigerate until thickened.

2 Heat oven to 200°F. Line cookie sheet with cooking parchment paper. In medium bowl, beat egg whites with electric mixer on medium speed until soft peaks form. Gradually add ⅓ cup granulated sugar, beating on high speed just until stiff peaks form. Fold in ⅓ cup powdered sugar.

3 In small bowl, mix ¼ cup powdered sugar and the cocoa. Fold cocoa mixture, ⅓ at a time, into beaten egg whites. Spoon mixture into decorating bag fitted with star tip. Pipe into 24 (1½-inch) rounds, about 1 inch apart, on parchment paper.

4 Bake 1 hour to 1 hour 15 minutes or until crisp. Slide parchment paper with cookies onto cooling rack. Cool completely, about 5 minutes.

5 For each sandwich cookie, spread chilled ganache on flat side of 1 meringue; top with second meringue. Meringue becomes tough if it absorbs moisture; store in a loosely covered container at room temperature. If the humidity is high, transfer to a tightly covered container.

High Altitude (3500–6500 ft): Decrease granulated sugar to ¼ cup. Heat oven to 225°F. Bake 1 hour 15 minutes to 1 hour 30 minutes.

■■■ **take note:** Meringues that are the same size look better when sandwiched together, and it's easy to make them the same size. Just trace 1½-inch circles on the parchment paper; turn the paper over and pipe the meringue on the other side within the circles.

1 Sandwich Cookie: Calories 130; Total Fat 7g (Saturated Fat 4.5g; Trans Fat 0g); Cholesterol 10mg; Sodium 25mg; Total Carbohydrate 14g (Dietary Fiber 1g) **Exchanges:** 1 Other Carbohydrate, 1½ Fat **Carbohydrate Choices:** 1

chocolate-coconut thumbprint cookies

Prep Time: 1 Hour 5 Minutes
Start to Finish: 1 Hour 35 Minutes

About 3 dozen cookies

>>

- **1 roll (16.5 oz) refrigerated sugar cookies**
- **4 oz sweet baking chocolate, melted, cooled 10 minutes**
- **2 tablespoons all-purpose flour**
- **½ cup flaked coconut**
- **½ cup coconut pecan creamy ready-to-spread frosting (from 1-lb container)**
- **2 oz sweet baking chocolate, chopped**
- **½ teaspoon vegetable oil**

1 Heat oven to 350°F. In large bowl, break up cookie dough. Using hands, stir or knead in 4 oz melted chocolate and the flour until well blended. Divide dough in half; cover and refrigerate one half until ready to use.

2 Shape remaining half into 18 balls. Place coconut in shallow dish; dip half of each ball in coconut to coat. On ungreased cookie sheets, place balls, coconut sides up, 1 inch apart. Repeat with remaining half of dough.

3 Bake 7 to 9 minutes or until edges are set and centers are almost set. Immediately make indentation in center of each cookie with end of wooden spoon. Fill each indentation with ½ teaspoon frosting. Cool 2 minutes; remove from cookie sheets to cooling racks. Cool about 30 minutes or until set.

4 In small microwavable bowl, microwave 2 oz chocolate and the oil uncovered on High about 1 minute 30 seconds or until chocolate is softened; stir until melted and smooth. Drizzle chocolate over cookies.

High Altitude (3500–6500 ft): Bake 9 to 11 minutes.

Chocolate-Hazelnut Thumbprint Cookies: Substitute ½ cup hazelnut spread with cocoa (from 13-oz jar) for the coconut pecan frosting.

Chocolate-Berry Thumbprint Cookies: Substitute ½ cup red raspberry or strawberry seedless jam or jelly for the coconut pecan frosting. Stir the jam or jelly until smooth before filling the cookies.

1 Cookie: Calories 110; Total Fat 5g (Saturated Fat 2g; Trans Fat 1g); Cholesterol 0mg; Sodium 50mg; Total Carbohydrate 14g (Dietary Fiber 0g) **Exchanges:** 1 Other Carbohydrate, 1 Fat **Carbohydrate Choices:** 1

orange and pine nut thumbprints

Prep Time: 50 Minutes
Start to Finish: 50 Minutes

About 2 dozen cookies

¾ **cup pine nuts, finely chopped**
3 tablespoons honey
1 tablespoon orange juice
½ **cup butter or margarine,**
softened
¼ **cup packed brown sugar**
1 teaspoon grated orange peel
1 teaspoon vanilla
1 egg yolk
1 cup all-purpose flour
¼ **teaspoon salt**
¼ **cup orange marmalade**

1 Heat oven to 350°F. Line cookie sheets with cooking parchment paper. Place pine nuts in small bowl. In another small bowl, mix honey and orange juice until well blended. Set aside.

2 In medium bowl, beat butter and brown sugar with electric mixer on medium speed until fluffy. Beat in orange peel, vanilla and egg yolk until well blended. On low speed, beat in flour and salt until dough begins to stick together.

3 Shape dough into 1-inch balls. If necessary, flour hands for easier handling. Roll balls in honey mixture, then roll in pine nuts. Place 2 inches apart on cookie sheets. With thumb, make indentation in center of each cookie.

4 Bake 9 to 12 minutes or until cookies are set and edges are golden brown. Remove parchment paper with cookies from cookie sheets to cooling racks. Fill each cookie with ½ teaspoon marmalade. Remove cookies from paper.

High Altitude (3500–6500 ft): Increase flour to 1 cup plus 2 tablespoons.

■■■ **take note:** This recipe is a variation of a cookie popular in Provence, a region in southeastern France. Pine nuts, orange and honey are common ingredients in the cooking of the Mediterranean region. You can use ¾ cup finely chopped almonds instead of the pine nuts, if you prefer.

1 Cookie: Calories 110; Total Fat 7g (Saturated Fat 3g; Trans Fat 0g); Cholesterol 20mg; Sodium 55mg; Total Carbohydrate 12g (Dietary Fiber 0g) **Exchanges:** ½ Starch, 1½ Fat **Carbohydrate Choices:** 1

walnut logs

Prep Time: 1 Hour 15 Minutes
Start to Finish: 1 Hour 15 Minutes

About 3 dozen cookies

1 cup butter or margarine,
    softened
½ cup powdered sugar
1 teaspoon vanilla
2¼ cups all-purpose flour
¼ teaspoon salt
¾ cup finely chopped walnuts
2 oz semisweet baking chocolate,
    chopped

1 Cookie: Calories 110; Total Fat 7g (Saturated Fat 3.5g; Trans Fat 0g); Cholesterol 15mg; Sodium 55mg; Total Carbohydrate 9g (Dietary Fiber 0g) **Exchanges:** ½ Starch, 1½ Fat **Carbohydrate Choices:** ½

1   Heat oven to 375°F. In medium bowl, beat butter and powdered sugar with electric mixer on medium speed until creamy. Beat in vanilla. On low speed, beat in flour and salt until mixture is crumbly. Stir in ½ cup of the walnuts.

2   Shape dough into walnut-size balls; roll each into 3×¾-inch log. Place on ungreased cookie sheets.

3   Bake 9 to 12 minutes or until set and bottoms are golden brown. Immediately remove from cookie sheets to cooling racks. Cool completely, about 10 minutes.

4   Meanwhile, in small microwavable bowl, microwave chocolate uncovered on High 30 seconds; stir until smooth.

5   Place cooled cookies on sheet of waxed paper. Drizzle chocolate over cookies; sprinkle with remaining ¼ cup walnuts.

High Altitude (3500–6500 ft): No change.

Pecan Logs: Substitute ¾ cup finely chopped pecans for the walnuts and 2 oz. white chocolate baking bars, chopped, for the semisweet baking chocolate.

more any occasion cookies

cinnamon tea cakes

Prep Time: 1 Hour
Start to Finish: 1 Hour

About 4½ dozen cookies

COOKIES
1 cup butter or margarine,
  softened
½ cup powdered sugar
1 teaspoon vanilla
2 cups all-purpose flour
1 cup finely chopped or ground
  walnuts
½ teaspoon ground cinnamon
⅛ teaspoon salt

COATING
¼ cup granulated sugar
1 teaspoon ground cinnamon

1 Heat oven to 325°F. In large bowl, beat butter, powdered sugar and vanilla with electric mixer on medium speed until light and fluffy. On low speed, beat in flour, walnuts, ½ teaspoon cinnamon and the salt until well blended.

2 Shape dough into 1-inch balls. On ungreased cookie sheets, place balls 1 inch apart.

3 Bake 14 to 16 minutes or until set but not brown. Immediately remove from cookie sheets to cooling racks. Cool slightly, about 3 minutes.

4 Meanwhile, in small bowl, mix coating ingredients. Roll warm cookies in coating. Cool completely, about 15 minutes. Cookies can be placed in an airtight container and freeze up to 3 weeks. Before serving, thaw the cookies and reroll them in additional cinnamon-sugar mixture.

High Altitude (3500–6500 ft): No change.

■■■ **take note:** Use a small or mini food processor to grind the nuts. Pulse the nuts until they are fine pieces, being careful not to overprocess them to a powder because they will become too oily.

1 Cookie: Calories 70; Total Fat 4.5g (Saturated Fat 2.5g; Trans Fat 0g); Cholesterol 10mg; Sodium 30mg; Total Carbohydrate 6g (Dietary Fiber 0g) **Exchanges:** ½ Other Carbohydrate, 1 Fat **Carbohydrate Choices:** ½

spiced almond-chocolate crinkles

Prep Time: 2 Hours
Start to Finish: 3 Hours

About 5 dozen cookies

¼ cup butter or margarine
4 oz unsweetened baking
    chocolate, cut into pieces
4 eggs
2 cups all-purpose flour
2 cups granulated sugar
½ cup chopped almonds
2 teaspoons baking powder
½ teaspoon salt
½ teaspoon ground ginger
½ teaspoon ground cinnamon
¼ teaspoon ground cloves
¾ cup powdered sugar

1 In 3-quart saucepan, melt butter and chocolate over low heat, stirring constantly, until smooth. Remove from heat. Cool slightly, about 5 minutes.

2 With spoon, beat eggs into chocolate mixture until well blended. Beat in remaining ingredients except powdered sugar until well blended. Cover dough with plastic wrap; refrigerate at least 1 hour for easier handling.

3 Heat oven to 300°F. Spray cookie sheets with cooking spray. Place powdered sugar in small bowl. Shape dough into 1-inch balls; roll in powdered sugar, coating heavily. Place balls 2 inches apart on cookie sheets.

4 Bake 13 to 18 minutes or until set. Immediately remove from cookie sheets to cooling racks.

High Altitude (3500–6500 ft): No change.

Chocolate-Almond Crinkles: Omit ginger, cinnamon and cloves. Add 1 teaspoon almond extract and 1 teaspoon vanilla.

1 Cookie: Calories 80; Total Fat 2.5g (Saturated Fat 1.5g; Trans Fat 0g); Cholesterol 15mg; Sodium 45mg; Total Carbohydrate 12g (Dietary Fiber 0g) **Exchanges:** 1 Other Carbohydrate, ½ Fat **Carbohydrate Choices:** 1

fresh ginger–pumpkin tassies

Prep Time: 35 Minutes
Start to Finish: 1 Hour 35 Minutes

2 dozen cookies

CRUST
1¼ cups all-purpose flour
½ cup butter or margarine, softened
1 package (3 oz) cream cheese, softened

FILLING
¾ cup packed brown sugar
½ cup canned pumpkin (not pumpkin pie mix)
3 tablespoons half-and-half
1 teaspoon grated gingerroot
½ teaspoon vanilla
1 egg

TOPPING
¼ cup all-purpose flour
2 tablespoons packed brown sugar
1 tablespoon butter or margarine, softened

1 Heat oven to 350°F. In large bowl, beat crust ingredients with electric mixer on medium speed until well blended. Shape dough into 24 (1¼-inch) balls. Place 1 ball in each of 24 ungreased miniature muffin cups; press in bottom and up side of each cup, level with tops of cups.

2 In medium bowl, mix filling ingredients until well blended. Spoon slightly less than 1 tablespoon filling into each crust-lined cup. In small bowl, mix topping ingredients until crumbly. Carefully sprinkle 1 teaspoon topping over each filled cup.

3 Bake 18 to 22 minutes or until puffed and tip of knife inserted in center comes out clean. Immediately run knife around edges of cookies. Cool cookies in pans 5 minutes. Carefully remove cookies from muffin cups to cooling racks. Cool completely, about 30 minutes.

High Altitude (3500–6500 ft): Bake 18 to 24 minutes.

■■■ **take note:** Leftover gingerroot? Tightly wrap unpeeled gingerroot, and refrigerate it up to 3 weeks or freeze it up to 6 months. Just grate the amount of frozen gingerroot you need, and return the rest to the freezer.

1 Cookie: Calories 120; Total Fat 6g (Saturated Fat 3.5g; Trans Fat 0g); Cholesterol 25mg; Sodium 50mg; Total Carbohydrate 14g (Dietary Fiber 0g) **Exchanges:** 1 Starch, 1 Fat **Carbohydrate Choices:** 1

mint truffle cups

Prep Time: 35 Minutes
Start to Finish: 2 Hours 40 Minutes

2 dozen cookies

CRUST
½ **cup powdered sugar**
½ **cup butter or margarine,**
   softened
1 egg
1 cup all-purpose flour
¼ **cup unsweetened baking cocoa**

FILLING
⅔ **cup semisweet chocolate chips**
½ **cup whipping cream**
¼ **teaspoon peppermint extract**

TOPPING
12 thin rectangular crème de
   menthe chocolate candies,
   unwrapped, coarsely chopped

1 In medium bowl, beat powdered sugar and butter with electric mixer on medium speed until light and fluffy. Beat in egg until well blended. On low speed, beat in flour and cocoa until well blended. Cover with plastic wrap; refrigerate 1 to 2 hours for easier handling.

2 Heat oven to 325°F. Divide dough into 24 equal pieces. Place 1 piece in each of 24 ungreased miniature muffin cups; press in bottom and up side of each cup, level with tops of cups.

3 Bake 13 to 16 minutes or until set. Cool in pans on cooling racks 20 minutes. Remove from pans.

4 Meanwhile, in 2-quart saucepan, heat filling ingredients over low heat, stirring constantly, until chocolate is melted and smooth. Remove from heat. Cool about 20 minutes or until filling thickens slightly.

5 Spoon about 2 teaspoons filling into each baked chocolate cup. Refrigerate at least 30 minutes until filling is set. Sprinkle chopped candies on top of each cookie; press in lightly. Store covered in refrigerator. Remove from refrigerator about 30 minutes before serving.

High Altitude (3500–6500 ft): Bake 15 to 18 minutes.

■■■ **take note:** Be sure to use peppermint extract rather than mint extract because the mint flavor won't blend as well with the rest of the ingredients.

1 Cookie: Calories 120; Total Fat 8g (Saturated Fat 4.5g; Trans Fat 0g); Cholesterol 25mg; Sodium 35mg; Total Carbohydrate 11g (Dietary Fiber 0g) **Exchanges:** 1 Other Carbohydrate, 1½ Fat **Carbohydrate Choices:** 1

little almond sandwich cookies

Prep Time: 1 Hour 15 Minutes
Start to Finish: 1 Hour 15 Minutes

7½ *dozen sandwich cookies*

COOKIES

>> **1 roll (16.5 oz) refrigerated sugar cookies**
½ cup all-purpose flour
½ teaspoon almond extract
1 tablespoon granulated sugar

FILLING
2 cups powdered sugar
¼ cup butter or margarine, softened
4 teaspoons milk
¼ teaspoon almond extract
1 drop red food color

1 Heat oven to 350°F. In large bowl, break up cookie dough. Stir or knead in flour and almond extract until well blended.

2 Shape dough into 180 (½-inch) balls. On ungreased cookie sheets, place balls 1 inch apart. Press bottom of glass dipped into granulated sugar on each ball until ¼ inch thick; prick top of each with a fork.

3 Bake 6 to 8 minutes until set but not brown. Cool 1 minute; remove from cookie sheets to cooling racks. Cool completely, about 15 minutes.

4 Meanwhile, in small bowl, beat filling ingredients with electric mixer on low speed until smooth and creamy. Spread about 1 teaspoon filling on bottoms of half of the cookies. Top each with another cookie, bottom side down; press gently. Store covered in refrigerator.

High Altitude (3500–6500 ft): No change.

■■■ **take note:** You can easily cut this recipe in half if you don't want to make 7½ dozen cookies. Cut the roll of sugar cookie dough in half; tightly wrap one half and refrigerate to use later. Bake the cookies as directed on the package.

2 Sandwich Cookies: Calories 40; Total Fat 1.5g (Saturated Fat 0.5g; Trans Fat 0g); Cholesterol 0mg; Sodium 20mg; Total Carbohydrate 7g (Dietary Fiber 0g) **Exchanges:** ½ Starch **Carbohydrate Choices:** ½

my chai cookies

Prep Time: 45 Minutes
Start to Finish: 1 Hour

3 dozen cookies

>> **1 roll (16.5 oz) refrigerated sugar cookies**
¼ cup all-purpose flour
¼ cup finely chopped pecans
1 package (1 oz) vanilla or original-flavor chai tea latte mix
¾ cup powdered sugar

1 Heat oven to 350°F. In large bowl, break up cookie dough. Stir or knead in flour, pecans and 2 teaspoons of the chai tea mix until well blended.

2 Shape dough into 36 (1-inch) balls. On ungreased cookie sheets, place balls 1 inch apart.

3 Bake 11 to 15 minutes or until tops appear dry and edges just begin to brown. Cool 1 minute; remove from cookie sheets to cooling racks.

4 In shallow dish, mix remaining chai tea mix and the powdered sugar. Roll warm cookies in sugar mixture. Cool completely, about 15 minutes. Roll in powdered sugar mixture again.

High Altitude (3500–6500 ft): No change.

■■■ **take note:** These cookies use chai tea latte mix, which contains black tea, honey, spices and dried milk. Look for it near the other packages of tea.

1 Cookie: Calories 80; Total Fat 3.5g (Saturated Fat 0.5g; Trans Fat 0.5g); Cholesterol 0mg; Sodium 45mg; Total Carbohydrate 12g (Dietary Fiber 0g) **Exchanges:** 1 Other Carbohydrate, ½ Fat **Carbohydrate Choices:** 1

almond-anise biscotti

Prep Time: 30 Minutes
Start to Finish: 1 Hour 15 Minutes

About 40 cookies

½ **cup granulated sugar**
½ **cup packed brown sugar**
¼ **cup butter or margarine,**
  softened
1 **tablespoon anise seed**
3 **eggs**
3 **cups all-purpose flour**
1 **tablespoon baking powder**
½ **cup chopped almonds**

1 Heat oven to 350°F. Lightly spray cookie sheet with cooking spray.

2 In large bowl, beat granulated sugar, brown sugar and butter with electric mixer on medium speed until well blended. Beat in anise seed and eggs until well blended. On low speed, beat in flour and baking powder until well blended. Stir in almonds.

3 Divide dough in half; shape each half into 10×1-inch roll. Place rolls 4 inches apart on cookie sheet; flatten each to 2-inch width.

4 Bake 20 to 30 minutes or until golden brown. Cool completely, about 15 minutes. Cut each roll diagonally into ½-inch slices.

5 Arrange slices, cut sides down, on ungreased cookie sheets. Bake 6 to 10 minutes or until bottoms begin to brown; turn. Bake 3 to 5 minutes longer or until browned and crisp. Cool completely. Store in tightly covered container.

High Altitude (3500–6500 ft): No change.

Almond Biscotti: Omit anise seed. Add ½ teaspoon vanilla and ½ teaspoon almond extract with the eggs.

Chocolate-Almond Biscotti: Omit anise seed. Decrease flour to 2½ cups and almonds to ⅓ cup. Add ⅓ cup unsweetened baking cocoa with the flour.

Hazelnut Biscotti: Omit anise seed. Add 1 teaspoon vanilla with the eggs. Substitute ½ cup chopped hazelnuts (filberts) for the almonds.

■■■ **take note:** A bit of chocolate is a nice added touch to these crisp cookies. Heat 3 ounces semisweet baking chocolate or white chocolate baking bar and ½ teaspoon shortening until melted and smooth. Drizzle chocolate over cookies, or dip half of each cookie into melted chocolate. Biscotti best retains its crispness when stored in a tightly covered container.

1 Cookie: Calories 80; Total Fat 2.5g
(Saturated Fat 1g; Trans Fat 0g); Cholesterol
20mg; Sodium 50mg; Total Carbohydrate
13g (Dietary Fiber 0g) **Exchanges:** 1 Other
Carbohydrate, ½ Fat **Carbohydrate Choices:** 1

frosted ginger cookies

Prep Time: 1 Hour 20 Minutes
Start to Finish: 3 Hours 20 Minutes

About 3 dozen cookies

COOKIES
1 cup shortening
1 cup molasses
3 cups all-purpose flour
1½ teaspoons baking soda
½ teaspoon salt
½ teaspoon ground ginger
¼ teaspoon ground nutmeg
¼ teaspoon ground cloves

FROSTING
¾ cup water
1 envelope unflavored gelatin
¾ cup granulated sugar
¾ cup powdered sugar
¾ teaspoon baking powder
1 teaspoon vanilla

1 Cookie: Calories 140; Total Fat 6g (Saturated Fat 1.5g; Trans Fat 1g); Cholesterol 0mg; Sodium 100mg; Total Carbohydrate 22g (Dietary Fiber 0g) **Exchanges:** ½ Starch, 1 Other Carbohydrate, 1 Fat **Carbohydrate Choices:** 1½

1 In large bowl, beat shortening and molasses with electric mixer on medium speed until blended, scraping bowl occasionally. Stir in remaining cookie ingredients until well combined. Cover dough with plastic wrap; refrigerate at least 2 hours for easier handling.

2 Heat oven to 350°F. On well-floured surface, roll dough to ¼-inch thickness, using lightly floured rolling pin. Cut with floured 2½-inch round cookie cutter. On ungreased cookie sheets, place cutouts 1 inch apart.

3 Bake 6 to 9 minutes or until set. Cool 1 minute; remove from cookie sheets to cooling racks. Cool completely, about 10 minutes.

4 In 2-quart saucepan, mix water and gelatin; let stand 5 minutes. Stir in granulated sugar; heat to full rolling boil. Reduce heat to medium; simmer 10 minutes without stirring to 220°F on candy thermometer. Remove from heat. Add powdered sugar; beat with electric mixer on low speed until foamy. Add baking powder and vanilla; beat on low speed about 5 minutes or until glossy and spreadable.

5 Spread frosting on bottom of each cookie to within ⅛ inch of edge. Let stand about 2 hours until frosting is set before storing in tightly covered container to help prevent the frosting from becoming hard.

High Altitude (3500–6500 ft): No change.

■■■ **take note:** These cookies are based on the original Sally Ann Cookies, which had a rectangular shape. You can make the original shape by cutting the dough with an empty 7- or 12-ounce luncheon meat can that has both ends removed. The cooked frosting makes a "true" Sally Ann Cookie, but you can use vanilla creamy ready-to-spread frosting instead and still enjoy these gingery cookies.

maple leaf cream wafers

Prep Time: 55 Minutes
Start to Finish: 1 Hour 55 Minutes

About 3 dozen sandwich cookies

COOKIES
1 cup butter or margarine, softened
⅓ cup whipping cream
½ teaspoon maple flavor
2 cups all-purpose flour
2 tablespoons granulated sugar

FILLING
¼ cup butter or margarine, softened
1 cup powdered sugar
½ teaspoon maple flavor
3 to 4 teaspoons milk

1 In large bowl, stir 1 cup butter, the whipping cream and ½ teaspoon maple flavor until well blended. Stir in flour until well blended. Divide dough in half; shape each half into flattened disk. Wrap each disk in plastic wrap; refrigerate 1 hour for easier handling.

2 Heat oven to 375°F. On lightly floured surface, roll half of dough at a time to ⅛-inch thickness, using lightly floured rolling pin. (Keep remaining half of dough refrigerated.) Cut dough with 2-inch maple leaf–shape cookie cutter. On ungreased cookie sheets, place cutouts 1 inch apart. Sprinkle with granulated sugar. Prick each cookie 3 or 4 times with fork.

3 Bake 7 to 10 minutes or until slightly puffed and edges are light golden brown. Cool 1 minute; remove from cookie sheets to cooling racks. Cool completely, about 10 minutes.

4 In small bowl, mix filling ingredients, adding enough milk until smooth and spreadable; beat until smooth. Spread slightly less than 1 teaspoon filling between 2 cookies.

High Altitude (3500–6500 ft): Decrease butter in cookies to ¾ cup. Bake 9 to 11 minutes.

■■■ **take note:** You can bake the cookies and prepare the filling up to 2 days in advance. Store the cooled cookies in a tightly covered container at room temperature. Cover and refrigerate the filling. Bring the filling to room temperature and assemble the sandwiches just before serving.

1 Sandwich Cookie: Calories 110; Total Fat 7g (Saturated Fat 4.5g; Trans Fat 0g); Cholesterol 20mg; Sodium 45mg; Total Carbohydrate 9g (Dietary Fiber 0g) **Exchanges:** ½ Starch, 1½ Fat **Carbohydrate Choices:** ½

helpful nutrition and cooking information

Nutrition Guidelines

We provide nutrition information for each recipe that includes calories, fat (saturated and trans), cholesterol, sodium, total carbohydrate, dietary fiber, exchanges and carbohydrate choices. Individual food choices can be based on this information.

Recommended intake for a daily diet of 2,000 calories as set by the Food and Drug Administration

Total Fat	Less than 65g
Saturated Fat	Less than 20g
Cholesterol	Less than 300mg
Sodium	Less than 2,400mg
Total Carbohydrate	300g
Dietary Fiber	25g

Criteria Used for Calculating Nutrition Information

- The first ingredient was used wherever a choice is given (such as ⅓ cup sour cream or plain yogurt).

- The first ingredient amount was used wherever a range is given (such as ½ to 1 cup chopped nuts).

- The first serving number was used wherever a range is given (such as 4 to 6 servings).

- "If desired" ingredients and recipe variations were not included (such as sprinkle with brown sugar, if desired).

Ingredients Used in Recipe Testing and Nutrition Calculations

- Ingredients used for testing represent those that the majority of consumers use in their homes such as large eggs, 2% milk, and all-purpose flour.

- Fat-free, low-fat or low-sodium products were not used, unless otherwise indicated.

- Cooking spray, baking spray with flour or vegetable shortening (not butter or margarine) was used to grease pans, unless otherwise indicated.

Equipment Used in Recipe Testing

We use equipment for testing that the majority of consumers use in their homes. If a specific piece of equipment (such as a wire whisk) is necessary for recipe success, it is listed in the recipe.

- Cookware and bakeware without nonstick coatings were used, unless otherwise indicated.

- No dark-colored, black or insulated bakeware was used.

- When a pan is specified in a recipe, a metal pan was used; a baking dish or pie plate means ovenproof glass was used.

- An electric hand mixer was used for mixing only when mixer speeds are specified in the recipe directions. When a mixer speed is not given, a spoon or fork was used.

metric conversion guide

Volume

U.S. UNITS	CANADIAN METRIC	AUSTRALIAN METRIC
¼ teaspoon	1 mL	1 ml
½ teaspoon	2 mL	2 ml
1 teaspoon	5 mL	5 ml
1 tablespoon	15 mL	20 ml
¼ cup	50 mL	60 ml
⅓ cup	75 mL	80 ml
½ cup	125 mL	125 ml
⅔ cup	150 mL	170 ml
¾ cup	175 mL	190 ml
1 cup	250 mL	250 ml
1 quart	1 liter	1 liter
1½ quarts	1.5 liters	1.5 liters
2 quarts	2 liters	2 liters
2½ quarts	2.5 liters	2.5 liters
3 quarts	3 liters	3 liters
4 quarts	4 liters	4 liters

weight

U.S. UNITS	CANADIAN METRIC	AUSTRALIAN METRIC
1 ounce	30 grams	30 grams
2 ounces	55 grams	60 grams
3 ounces	85 grams	90 grams
4 ounces (¼ pound)	115 grams	125 grams
8 ounces (½ pound)	225 grams	225 grams
16 ounces (1 pound)	455 grams	500 grams
1 pound	455 grams	½ kilogram

measurements

INCHES	CENTIMETERS
1	2.5
2	5.0
3	7.5
4	10.0
5	12.5
6	15.0
7	17.5
8	20.5
9	23.0
10	25.5
11	28.0
12	30.5
13	33.0

temperatures

FAHRENHEIT	CELSIUS
32°	0°
212°	100°
250°	120°
275°	140°
300°	150°
325°	160°
350°	180°
375°	190°
400°	200°
425°	220°
450°	230°
475°	240°
500°	260°

NOTE: The recipes in this cookbook have not been developed or tested using metric measures. When converting recipes to metric, some variations in quality may be noted.

index

Note: Numbers in *italics* indicate photos

Hungry for more?
See what else Pillsbury has to offer.

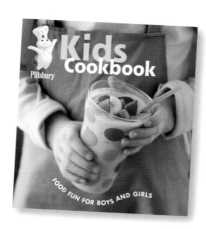